HELLO
STRANGER

ALSO BY MANUEL BETANCOURT

The Male Gazed

Judy Garland's "Judy at Carnegie Hall"

Musings on Modern Intimacies

HELLO
STRANGER

MANUEL BETANCOURT

Catapult
New York

HELLO STRANGER

"In Memory of My Feelings," "Homosexuality," "On Rachmaninoff's Birthday ['I am so glad that Larry Rivers made a...'}," and "Two Dreams of Waking" from *The Collected Poems of Frank O'Hara* by Frank O'Hara, copyright © 1971 by Maureen Granville-Smith, Administratrix of the Estate of Frank O'Hara, copyright renewed 1999 by Maureen O'Hara Granville-Smith and Donald Allen. Used by permission of Alfred A. Knopf, an imprint of the Knopf Doubleday Publishing Group, a division of Penguin Random House LLC. All rights reserved.

First Catapult edition: 2025

ISBN: 978-1-64622-229-2

Library of Congress Control Number: 2024943547

Jacket design by Farjana Yasmin
Jacket art © John Gress / Getty Images
Book design by Laura Berry
Door photograph © Happyphotons / Adobe Stock

Catapult
New York, NY
books.catapult.co

Printed in the United States of America

10 9 8 7 6 5 4 3 2 1

To the disarming Natalie Portman,
for making the idea of this book possible.

And to JAM, for making the emotional truth of it a reality.

CONTENTS

HELLO
STRANGER

1.
HELLO

"HELLO, STRANGER."

As an opener, you really can't ask for better. How tantalizing to imagine how, why, and—crucially—to whom one would address such a line. There's a familiarity to our use of these two words that somehow also depends on estrangement and distance. A stranger, after all, requires no such explicit recognition. You'd only greet someone that way if your aim was to make them strangers no more. There's an immediate pull toward closeness, toward intimacy. Toward narrative, in fact. Toward a series of events that will dispel any sense of *un*familiarity. There's a winking knowingness in such a greeting. Aptly deployed, it's as potent a come-on as one can muster, the start of a flirtation where the tacit understanding is that there's a thrill in beckoning a total stranger toward you, the better to acquaint yourself with them in more delightfully delectable ways.

My fascination with the narrative and flirtatious possibilities of those two words comes from the place where I've long purloined many of my most head-spinning obsessions: the movies. One movie, to be exact. "Hello, stranger" is the very first line of dialogue in Mike Nichols's 2004 drama *Closer*. A young woman with haphazardly dyed short red hair, donning a ratty jacket and little to no makeup, has just been run over. Gently hit, actually. Having fainted soon after the collision, she comes to and stares at the handsome bloke who'd caught her eye before she attempted to cross a London street. He's concerned, yes. But intrigued above all else by this wily-looking bird. Her eyes alight upon his and, as if nothing of consequence had just happened to explain the blood on her forehead and on her leg, she punctuates her greeting with a knowing smile. Nichols's camera rightfully keeps us focused on Alice, played by Natalie Portman, so that when she's looking straight into Dan (that'd be Jude Law), we're made to feel like she's talking to us as well. We're immediately interpolated by her words, made to feel like strangers who are nevertheless being asked to be more. Like Dan, a bumbling obituarist who can't believe his luck when he gets to play knight in shining armor for this wayward American damsel, escorting her to the hospital where she'll be stitched up, we're smitten right from the start. I was, at least. All with the power of two words delivered in the figure of a flinty, flirty stranger.

As someone who's been obsessed with Tennessee Williams's *A Streetcar Named Desire* for as long as I can remember, there's always been something alluring about strangers—especially, like Blanche DuBois says in that play, those on whose kindness I could and have always depended on. That is to say, while I understand the impulse toward demonizing strangers with catchy, parent-ready rhyming warnings, I've come to wonder what it might mean to embrace, instead, the very possibilities such figures can inspire in us. I need only think of the many morning commutes on subway trains (and NJ Transit ones, at that) where a mere glance from a fetching man across from me could and did send me into hypothetical rabbit holes where I'd imagine how I could push past my own self-consciousness (not to mention awkward shyness) so as to kick-start a conversation that would lead to a number, to a date, to a future. Or maybe even just to a kiss, to a bed, to a fling. In my twenties, the closest I ever got to making such a scene happen was once at a theater where a dashing moviegoer who'd caught my eye as we both lined up for some indie film began inching toward me. He smiled my way and, quite bashfully, asked for my number. Only, since I'd moved to the States but a few weeks prior, I hadn't yet memorized my new U.S. cell number. As I stumbled through those ten digits to the best of my ability, I saw his interest dwindle. Rightly thinking I was conjuring up a fake number in real time and doing a poor job of it, he just as quickly retreated to his group of friends. He never did text or call.

As my endless daydreaming about fellow subway riders and moviegoers suggests, no broad concept of "the stranger" can be uncoupled from our ideas about romance and desire. How we think about couples, in fact. And, I'll add (because I am nothing if not an English major at heart), about narratives. Love stories, after all, are essentially tales about turning strangers into kin; they encourage us to view those we don't know and have just met as instant possible matches. Not as figures to be feared but ones to be entranced by.

In his seminal 1908 essay, "The Stranger," one of the most influential pieces of early twentieth-century thinking about this very concept, Georg Simmel suggests that what made "the stranger" such fertile ground for sociological investigation was the way it functioned as a synthesis of closeness and distance, of detachment and engagement. He writes, "The stranger is a paradox: he is here, close at hand, but his having recently been far away is also present to us." They may never (or not just yet) be folded into the social fabric. But even if they are, their foreignness, their feeling of having been elsewhere, remains. Simmel's is a study on a sociological level— about in- and out-groups, about the social valence of those we do not consider kin. The stranger becomes, in his telling, a way to limit who is known, who belongs. And who is considered an outsider. But curiously, he also acknowledges how said figure can function within more intimate relations, erotic ones in particular. "A trace of strangeness lingers in even the most intimate relationships," he suggests, arguing that when one is in that first flush of passion with another (say, when you've caught their eye after they've been in an accident), you're convinced about its uniqueness (how could you possibly be so lucky?). It's only once you get past that, once an intimacy is further entrenched, that estrangement sets in. This sounds counterintuitive. Especially because we often imagine getting to know someone else to organically lead toward *more* intimacy, not less. Yet Simmel understands that we may feel most unlike ourselves with those we spend the most time with. He also ties it to the sense that once the initial spark dissipates, you realize that the intimacy you've come to nurture isn't (can't really be) unique, your own. Surely many others have similarly chanced upon such a story, such intimacy: no matter how close you've become with that once-stranger, there will always be a kind of distance between you—for if it hadn't been them, it would've been someone else. There's always room to reveal more of yourself to others. This is a story as old as time and its specificity is only novel at the start. And so your mind cannot help but acknowledge that there may be no such uniqueness to your experience, to your relationship. And, more to the point, you're forced to admit that "if one had not accidentally encountered this particular person, many others might have gained a similar importance for us instead." The inkling of such estrangement, Simmel notes, is tied to the ways in which those other possibilities (no matter how unrealizable) hover over your relationship: "They creep from each particular act of naming like a fog that still has to merge into a definite shape, a shape we might call jealousy."

Simmel doesn't spend much more than a paragraph on these ideas about the indefinite number of strangers you *didn't* encounter (or won't or have yet to pursue), and how they remain key in understanding your individually realized relationship. But they offer an opening as to how to think about estrangement, closeness, and intimacy as irrevocably tied together—especially within the realm of romance, within the realm of romantic narratives.

A stranger is always a beginning. A *potential* beginning. In the genre of romance, in the world of those who are die-hard romantics, you're always one chance encounter away from kick-starting your very own love story. Here's why Dan and Alice's meeting has stayed with me for close to twenty years. On the face of it, we're basically in a welcome (and familiar) "meet-cute," replete with scintillating flirtatious conversations to match. Yet the more you tease it out—as I have done for two decades now, obsessed as I remain with this most titillating encounter—the more you realize that the push toward closeness between this young bird and this dashing lad is rife with reticence, as if they each knew the only way to reveal themselves to the other was through a performed sense of intimacy.

"Hello, stranger," then, nudges me to think not only of Simmel's probing considerations on how social groups define themselves by what and who they are not, but of his extended treatise on that most playful of interactions between yourself and a stranger. That's because decades after publishing "The Stranger," Simmel turned his attention to the practice that figure feels best suited for. "Flirtation" was part of a larger project, *On Women, Sexuality, and Love*. Blinkered as his rigidly held gendered ideas were, Simmel was nevertheless fascinated by the social possibilities of flirtation, especially when uncoupled from, say, seduction. There's a gleeful aimlessness in flirting that, as he argued back in 1923, pushes back against the teleology we ascribe to romantic love. That is, where stories of "boy meets girl" are forcefully driven into "boy gets girl" and eventually "boy marries girl" (that socially sanctioned happily ever after), flirtation allows interactions to flirt, instead, with endless possibilities. "Flirtation has this cachet of the provisional, of suspension and indecision," he writes.

To flirt is to start a story that may have nothing but a beginning. Paul Fleming, in revisiting Simmel's work this century, notes that this is precisely what makes flirtation such a thrilling and tautological social dynamic that's hard to apprehend in the way we do other types of interpersonal interactions: "One flirts with someone in order to flirt with someone and thus enjoy the pleasing effect of this free, disinterested play," he writes. "Coquetry is an end-in-itself and thus without end." Flirtation could be an endless loop if only we'd let it. This is because of what's at the heart of such a dynamic. For Simmel, the flirt (always a woman, in his view) is pulling you in and pushing you away simultaneously: "The distinctiveness of the flirt," he argues, "lies in the fact that she awakens delight and desire by means of a unique antithesis and synthesis: through the alternation or simultaneity of accommodation and denial; by a symbolic, allusive assent and dissent." She wants you, or seems to want you, and still she keeps her distance. The key gestures of the flirt—the coy smile, the look askance, the blush—are all modes with which we attract attention while also giving ourselves room to deny it. All are ways to avoid precisely what flirtation disavows: commitment.

As Adam Phillips argues in *On Flirtation* (published seven decades after Simmel's own essay on the subject), "To be committed to something—a person, an ideology, a vocabulary, a way of going about things—one has first to be committed, perhaps unconsciously, to commitment itself." Inadvertently, it would seem, we are wedded to the very notion *of* commitment and struggle to tell stories (let alone imagine relationships and even lives) that aren't anchored, weighted, or otherwise tied to our capacity for commitment (or a specific *kind* of sexual and romantic commitment). Which is another way of saying that we're constantly looking to turn moments into beginnings so that we can have (or envision, at least) endings: "In flirtation you never know whether the beginning of the story—the story of the relationship—will be the end; flirtation, that is to say, exploits the idea of surprise." Surprise, of course, is hard to sustain. Such a feeling depends on its own ephemerality; it doesn't quite have the stable shelf life of a word and a concept like "commitment." But there's a thrill there as well, especially if we're looking for avenues of thought that move us away from the familiar.

Flirtation hinges on a moment where your life could suddenly splinter into any number of outcomes, into any number of stories. Flirtation, thus, is a site of possibility; it's a kind of suspended state of animation where your world sits at a standstill. "Flirtation, if it can be sustained," Phillips adds, "is a way of cultivating wishes, of playing for time." That's a big *if* right there. And the key, of course, to flirtation's allure. What is flirtation if not the ultimately subjunctive mood, an *if* in and of itself? To flirt is to create an opening to look at those many unrealized possibilities Simmel discusses in "The Stranger." To this end I'd like to posit that *Closer*, based on Patrick Marber's play by the same name, is ultimately a piece about flirtation, about its joys and its dangers. Namely, about what happens when flirts find themselves in stories that require endings, which is to say in the world of love and romance we've so constructed that leaves little room for play without requisite repercussions. After being a personal favorite for decades, *Closer* has become a site of emotional and intellectual interrogation for what we might learn about ourselves if we paid attention to what flirting with strangers, not to mention flirting with the idea of flirtation itself, can unlock within us, in ways both intimate and social, both personal and cultural.

I was in a small theater in Vancouver when I first fell for Portman's Alice (that's the name she gives Dan once they head out of the hospital and walk around Postman's Park before he leaves for work). Having come out to my mom (and friends and acquaintances) but one year before, and armed with my very first boyfriend, I walked into that theater with as assured a sense of self as I could've mustered as a college kid in his early twenties. Still in that itinerant bliss that washes over all such college flings, this boyfriend and I had developed a welcome movie-watching rhythm that had us alternate between Blockbuster rentals at his place and indie flicks at nearby theaters. We arrived at a screening of *Closer* with different kinds of apprehensions. The week before, he had taken me to see an outlandish documentary on quantum physics and philosophy aptly titled *What the #$*! Do We (K)now!?* I'd gritted my teeth through most of its pseudo pop psych mishmash even as I gathered that he'd really enjoyed the big questions about consciousness and connection this 2004 flick asked in (what I thought were) rather flippant ways. It was becoming clear we had decidedly different tastes and pop culture inclinations. And so, it was with a bit of trepidation that I insisted we catch *Closer* on opening weekend. The film, I argued, starred two of my favorite actresses. Joining Portman was Julia Roberts, the actress whose megawatt smile I tried to conjure whenever I self-consciously flashed my own.

Where my tall, lanky, and nerdy boyfriend looked to screens big and small for nourishing information about the world around him, for moments and conversations that helped him question why we were all here (he loved himself Big Topics up for debate), I had long turned to pop culture as a vehicle through which to understand myself and the minutiae of my everyday internal experience. He looked outward, I looked within. It was as much a difference in kind as in scale. Which is all to say I knew this dour drama about two interlocking couples in London who muse and embody a rather cynical version of modern romantic relationships was always going to be a hard sell. No matter. We were still in that honeymoon period where such differences were endearing rather than enraging. Catching him lovingly sniffing the sweater I'd left behind when I went to the restroom ahead of the trailers, for instance, felt like an adorable affectation that proved just how intoxicated he was with me. A reminder that, even as he'd once considered me much too forward (my flirting was obnoxiously performative for his tastes), I'd succeeded in getting him to date me after all. If I was at all apprehensive about where this budding if already quite domestic-driven relationship was going (we were a stay-at-home-and-cook-and-watch-movies rather than go-out-drinking-and-dancing-every-weekend kinda college couple), all that melted away when Portman locked eyes with the camera and enveloped me in what turned out to be one of the most affecting moviegoing experiences of my entire life.

Closer—and Alice in particular—felt like a warning. Structured as a series of duets between its four key characters (a former stripper, an obituarist, a photographer, and a doctor), the film is a bruising piece about the rotting roteness of long-term intimacy. And of the exhilarating thrills of strangers. Years later, I can now shamelessly admit that the brazenness of Alice's opening felt all too familiar. The coy gaze that demanded you come close even as it dared you to stay at a distance was not too different from the looks I'd been practicing in the mirror and artlessly throwing at various men in hopes they'd look at me with the flagrant desire I so coveted. I didn't tell my boyfriend at the time, but watching that first scene, scored as it is by Damien Rice's "The Blower's Daughter," took me back to the first time I ever laid eyes on him. As Rice sings about not being able to take his eyes off whomever he's crooning about, Dan and Alice catch each other's eyes across the crowded streets of

London. Similarly, when I'd first seen him at a college mixer hosted by the university's gay campus group, I'd been mesmerized. Back then there was (and sometimes there still is) something irresistible to me about self-conscious nerdy boys. It's the inner (and outer) nerd in me trying to find (sexy) kindred spirits. Not that many of my friends shared my fascination with him. But, cocky college kid that I was (or hoped to be), I made a point of trying to seduce him. That he seemed immune to my advances only made me try harder. When I look back at those arguably very clumsy attempts (which included inviting myself out to drinks with him and his friends and then making a laughable excuse to crash at his place, where he then proceeded to mock my put-on nonchalant attitude after coming out of his shower with a towel that I hoped left nothing to the imagination), I see a humbled twenty-year-old trying to hopelessly perform "sexiness." I was slim, lanky, and rather awkward. I could barely grow facial hair. I looked ever the twink, without any of the sexual confidence such a label can connote. When we finally started dating, it felt like a well-earned victory. Proof, perhaps, that my insecurities could finally be allayed. We'd gone from a meet-cute at a campus mixer toward an established romantic rhythm in what felt like record time, all of which, in my head, gave some structure to my sense of self as an out gay man. I was crafting a story worth living in, though one that required dimming down parts of myself that clearly did not cohere with this vision of prim and proper (and, ahem, monogamous) coupledom.

For one of the things I soon learned about myself shortly after coming out and coming into my own while studying abroad (I'd left my native Colombia for the rainy ways of the west coast of Canada) was that I was a shameless flirt. And, as it turns out, quite a skilled one. I'd practiced my quick-witted and decidedly not-safe-for-work banter in many an online forum and chat room in my late teens. My in-real-life attempts were never quite as smooth as my come-hither texting with men who craved to see, meet, and do plenty more in spaces where my own anonymity afforded me a boldness I always hoped to embody in real life. But soon enough, I found an intoxicating joy in getting strangers to look at me with a hunger I could just as easily egg on as dissipate at a moment's notice. It was that shamelessness that eventually got me in trouble with my boyfriend. What he at first imagined to be misplaced jealousy justly curdled into outright indignation after I came clean about an out-of-town indiscretion with a friend of mine. It was an instance of coy flirting gone much further than it should have, the first but not the last instance where my own baser instincts got the better of me and ruined what I'd told myself was a perfectly satisfying relationship.

If *Closer* had first felt like a warning, I soon turned the film into a balm. Here was a portrait of serial-monogamists-cum-cheaters who kept lying to each other and to themselves in order to get by. For as soon as Dan and Alice hit it off, the movie cuts to a year later when, in anticipation of the publication of a novel based on Alice's past as a stripper, Dan meets with a photographer (that'd be Roberts's Anna) for a respectable author headshot. Just as with Alice, he's instantly smitten. "You've ruined my life," he tells her with grating earnestness. He convinces himself that he can't help but pursue her, even when he knows the life he's built with Alice is exactly what he'd once desperately wanted. Soon enough, the film introduces Larry (Clive Owen), who falls for a woman named "Anna" he meets on the net and later still for the actual Anna he meets at an aquarium. The two date and later marry, but their domestic bliss comes crashing down once Anna confesses she's been seeing Dan for over a year. Each seduction feels like a fool's errand, as absurd and comic as it is inevitable and tragic. The film spirals toward a melancholy ending despite being structured by a string of scenes all brimming with possibility, all anchored on the thrilling practice of flirting. Alice and Dan flirt on the streets of London ("You came to," he tells her. "You focused on me. You said, 'Hello, stranger.'" "What a floozy!" she winks back). Anna and Dan coyly do so in her studio ("I don't kiss strange men," she goads him. "Neither do I," he responds before kissing her). Late one night on the net, Dan (passing himself off as a woman named "Anna") woos Dr. Larry ("Wear my wet knickers," he types), who then, in turn, woos Anna in real life ("You are bloody gorgeous," he coos). Lastly, in two scenes that bracket twinned breakup scenes, Larry and Alice playfully banter back and forth, first at an art gallery opening and months later at a strip club where she works.

The film is a chain-linked series of pas de deux between four strangers who love and hurt and lust and pine after each other for just as many years, itching to get closer to one another and yet finding in such performed intimacies only (or barely) cold comfort. It's no surprise that as an emotionally wounded twenty-year-old I would find in Nichols's adaptation a way through my first breakup, the big screen filled to the brim with lessons about how the very notion of building successful (honest!) long-term relationships was work. A lot of work, in fact.

When *Closer* first opened in 1997 at the Royal National Theatre in London, it cemented Marber's arrival as the heir apparent to the likes of David Mamet and Harold Pinter. The playwright, who'd gotten his start in stand-up and sketch comedy, had wowed UK audiences with 1995's *Dealer's Choice*, a very funny play that cribs from his own gambling addiction past to create a portrait of contemporary British masculinity. His dialogue in *Closer* is often brutal and sparse. He uses words like scalpels, whose surgical precision cuts and heals in equal measure, often within the same line. When Anna confesses to Dan that she slept with Larry in order to have him finally sign their divorce papers, he's dizzy with rancor. "Dan, please be bigger than . . . *jealous*," Anna begs him. "Please, be bigger." "What could be bigger than jealousy?" he spits back. The exchange, which Marber cut when adapting his script for the screen, offers a glimmer of the kind of hope that's buried within the play's many hurtful scenes: "*It hurts,*" Dan admits. "I'm ashamed. I know it's illogical and I do understand but *I hate you.* I love you and I don't like other men fucking you, is that so weird?" The question only feels rhetorical onstage because the audience no doubt agrees with puppyish, romantic Dan. It's so much easier to take his side than it is to understand, let alone endorse, Anna's aloof pragmatism. But that question is also an opening about the kind of couple they could be were Dan a little more imaginative. Were he, in his own words, a little more logical. A little less weird.

In *The Telegraph*, Charles Spencer raved that what he most loved about Marber's language was "that he gets right down to what Yeats described as 'the foul rag-and-bone shop of the heart.' Anyone who has loved and lost, anyone who has experienced infidelity or felt love die, will watch this play with stomach churning pangs of recognition." I certainly did. But the lessons I gathered about it when I was in my twenties look decidedly different from the ones I find in Marber's words these days. It's easy to watch Dan cheat on Alice and Anna cheat on Larry (and then Larry sleep with Alice and later again with Anna) and find little hope in Marber's vision of twentieth-century (and now twenty-first-century) romance. Two decades ago, I found solace in similarly fragile and fallible beings, characters who do know better and yet can't seem to do, let alone be, good. Their tenuous relationship with honesty ("What's so great about the truth? Try lying for a change. It's the currency of the world!") and with their unruly desires ("I fucked her to fuck you up!") bolstered my own sense of shame about my own emotional failures. But deep within (in between, you may say) those idyllic flirtatious moments and those bickering breakup scenes lies, I now believe, an opening to learn about how we narrativize our intimacies with those who are closest to us. But especially with those we've just met. The tragedy—and the romance, really—that occurs as Dan and Alice and Anna and Larry emotionally collide into one another lies in their inability to think outside of narrative, outside of well-worn tales about romance and heartache. All four are caught in stories they often wish they could shed, or rework, or recycle. Instead, they're stuck in a loop that will see them making the same mistakes over and over again, never learning enough about themselves or others.

Marber has long confessed that with *Closer* he wanted to make a play in the vein of *Sex, Lies, and Videotape*. The 1989 Steven Soderbergh Palme d'Or–winning film is best remembered as having helped usher in the independent film boom of the nineties. But beyond the industry-shattering, buzzy success this little indie that could enjoyed, *Sex, Lies, and Videotape* continues to amaze because, in film critic Peter Travers's words, it was and remains "an ardent, adult film" that so "incisively exposes the barriers we set up to avoid making contact." The film is about how costly it can be to connect, about the constricting ways we relate to one another, and about the emancipatory possibilities of the ephemeral intimacies we can construct with strangers. Like *Closer, Sex, Lies, and Videotape* centers on a quartet of characters: John and his wife, Ann (Peter Gallagher and Andie MacDowell); her sister, Cynthia (Laura San Giacomo); and Graham (James Spader), an old friend of John's who arrives to unsettle the furtive and fragile sexual triangle he unwittingly stumbles upon. As we learn early on, Cynthia is having an affair with John. Graham, who hasn't seen John in decades, is well armed to assess the situation: a drifter who's all too happy to move through the world with just one key (to his car), Spader's character is impotent by his own admission. The only way he can get off these days is by playing tapes he's made of women talking about their past sexual exploits. Said personal project is driven as much by curiosity as by a nurtured voyeuristic impulse that's taken over his entire sex drive. In fact, he's a voyeur of life, existing solely as a spectator of the world around him. He constantly opts to remain a cipher: better to be seen as a camera, as a gaze rather than subject or object of anyone else's desires.

Like *Closer, Sex, Lies, and Videotape* was somewhat autobiographical. The film was an attempt to exorcise elements of a past that Soderbergh was trying not to outrun. His film, he's said, is "all about people who will not say what they're thinking unless they're really pushed into a corner and poked." As the filmmaker spoke publicly with the press during its Cannes premiere, it dawned on him how alike the film and he were: "how much I'm still struggling with the distance I feel between myself and other people, and my feelings, and how difficult it still is for me to feel and not instantly analyze." The writer-director's breakout film flirted with the push and pull of distance and closeness, mining the immense chasm that can sometimes exist between who we are and who we want to be.

This, Soderbergh understood, was most acutely the case when we talk (and think and maybe even instantly analyze) sex. The schism between John and Ann is a sexual one: theirs is a mostly sexless marriage. "I've never really been into sex that much," Ann confesses to her therapist in the opening scene of the film. It's soon clear that all talk about sex makes her uncomfortable. But if she's able to keep herself buttoned up in her therapist's office (an intimate relationship that truly depends on an imbalanced sense of distance and closeness), it's her chats with carefree Graham that further rattle this angst-riddled housewife. Graham's openness about sex initially spooks the prim and proper Ann, who's resigned herself to not want or want for anything more (she can barely bring herself to masturbate and wonders aloud during therapy whether she's ever even had an orgasm). But the more time this unlikely pair spend together, the more Ann is forced to reckon with what she's kept at bay—eventually agreeing to take part in Graham's project, recording herself for his benefit. It's a decision that surprises and rankles Graham in equal measure, especially because it's driven by Ann's realization that Cynthia had already made a tape for him. Cynthia is a consummate flirt who clearly serves as a foil for Ann (one a sexually liberated young woman, the other a prudish young wife); it is through their contrast that Soderberg articulates our collective distinctions between socially sanctioned intimacies—and those, like the ones nurtured by Graham and Cynthia, that are pushed to the margins even as they feel like the most revealing of them all.

To watch *Sex, Lies, and Videotape* is not only to see *Closer*'s template but its inspiration distilled. It's not just that Marber hoped to create a nineties response to that late eighties flick where, say, the anonymous intimacy afforded by internet chat rooms echoed the disembodying potential of a camcorder. But that he wanted to create an equally raw and vulnerable love triangle turned square of sorts, where the very foundations of what we understand romantic and sexual relationships to be are violently upended. And at the heart of them both is the figure of the stranger. The videotapes are, it turns out, not only a way for Graham to get off but a way to keep the world and his desires at bay. He cherishes the intimacy he creates with his camera but wills himself not to act on it: what he most enjoys is the impersonal intimacy of it all. He finds closeness only in distance. When Cynthia, for instance, rushes back to his place and asks him to record her one more time, Graham refuses. "After the first time it's just not spontaneous," he tells her. "There's no edge anymore." That spontaneity (that surprise!) is what allows Graham to intimately know Cynthia (and later Ann), in ways neither sister let themselves be known to each other (and even to themselves).

Those questions, of how we can make ourselves known to strangers in ways we can't or dare not do with those closest to us is the structuring principle of Marber's *Closer*. In fact, that's what initially drew him to try to import Soderbergh's ideas onto the stage. Talking with Charlie Rose about a potential adaptation, Marber stressed, instead, why *Closer* was always conceived as a theatrical piece: "I think it's a better play than it could be a movie," he suggested. "Because it deals with very intimate subject matter. And having those intimacies expressed in front of a thousand people every night is enormously exciting, dramatically. Because the audience feels like they're privy to conversations that are entirely private." And yet actress Natasha Richardson saw the potential in adapting *Closer* into a film. She beamed during that Charlie Rose appearance, imagining the chance of playing Anna on the big screen and taking full advantage of the close-up so as to heighten the emotional tightrope she performed nightly at the Music Box Theatre for much of 1999. In fact, Richardson anticipated how Nichols would make ample use of the close-up to further highlight the pressing private intimacies Marber had dreamed up on page and stage alike. Like Anna, who spends her free time photographing strangers and hoping to capture their true selves (a blown-up close-up of a teary-eyed Alice becomes the centerpiece of her gallery show), *Closer* constantly captures its actors at a discomfiting distance, showing us every inch of their emotional breakdowns. But perhaps the most salient way in which Nichols, the best stage-to-screen adaptor of his generation, succeeded in transposing Marber's work was in similarly understanding how necessary it was to treat its relationships as equally hopeful and hopeless.

I've always thought *Closer* is a tad misunderstood as a film about romance. About love. Its tagline on promotional posters encouraged this: "If you believe in love at first sight, you never stop looking." Which in turn led writers like Richard Corliss at *Time* to hail it as a "love story for adults" (a pull quote that then found itself on the film's DVD cover). But there are no romantic arcs here, just a collection of lustful and vengeful fits and starts. Writing for *Variety*, Todd McCarthy insightfully argued that Marber is "uninterested in the quotidian of long-term relationships," clearly delineating instead "the beginnings of lust and the turning points that signal the end." And while the emotionally searing moments that capture how these various pairings collapse into themselves are a thrill to watch ("I don't love you anymore," Alice confesses to Dan late in the film. "Since when?" "Now. Just now," she quietly admits), I've long felt that *Closer* should instead be grappled with as an unparalleled examination of the promises and perils of the art of flirtation. Am I being intentionally hyperbolic? Obviously. But I can't think of many other films that so aggressively capture what it feels like to meet a stranger whose intoxicating fascination leads you to do (and think and daydream) things you'd never think possible. I mean, plenty of rom-coms start off this way; what is that first scene between Alice and Dan if not a classic meet-cute? But instead of narrativizing such moments into a larger story about how romance prevails, *Closer* incessantly goes to thornier and thornier places where the very structure of a "love story" plays out like a trap its characters cannot avoid. Clive Owen, who played Dan onstage before taking on the role of Larry in the film, understood the piece as such: Marber's work, he told an interviewer at the time of the film's release, "starts almost like a romantic comedy—witty and light—then slowly you're pulled into something deeply unsettling."

Part of what makes *Closer* such a distressing watch is how it unravels our socially sanctioned notions of what "love at first sight" moments are designed to set in motion. We often do ourselves a disservice in consigning scenes and stories about flirting to tales about love and relationships. This is precisely what foils Dan throughout and what Larry weaponizes against him. Seen this way, *Closer* becomes an amusing musing on the expansive possibilities strangers proffer us. But more to the point, the film becomes a trenchant indictment of the way we can estrange ourselves *from* ourselves when we let flirtatious moments be understood *only* as romantic beginnings— even, and especially, when they can only lead to disastrous endings. These are characters who cannot but see flirting as the start of a story rather than a narrative in it of itself. They're all eager to turn those moments of erotic recognition into something else, something more. At the expense, at times, of their own sense of self. Where would the drama in *Closer* be, say, if Dan didn't feel the need to pursue Alice and leave his linguist girlfriend, Ruth, behind? If he could be allowed to kiss strangers like Anna without immediately imagining that encounter as the start of a torrid yearslong affair? If he could understand Anna's decision to sleep with Larry in order to get him to sign their divorce papers, and be above the petty jealousy he can't shake off? Those narrative tensions, the very knotted twists that are the anchor points for each and every scene we're allowed to witness, are dependent on rigid ideas about how long-term relationships are supposed to work. About how romantic intimacies are codified. But they could just as easily be evaporated if only the hopeless romantic of the bunch (an obituarist turned failed novelist, naturally) weren't constantly dictating the very strictures he cannot let himself abide by.

Understood as a genre, romantic love is a self-starting narrative engine that is constantly propelled forward. Toward something. An engagement, say. Marriage, of course. Family and kids, even. Growing old together, ultimately. Long-term companionship depends on a teleological horizon. On, as Phillips so cannily argues, commitment itself. A commitment, he argues, that goes hand in hand with the rhetoric we use when we talk about love. Our languages of love, he notes, are versions of theology and epistemology. Our desires are driven by the desire to be known and understood (seen, even): in that first scene, Alice and Dan bond by slowly disclosing aspects of themselves that then become part of their love story. Including, crucially, the way he'd sized her up right away and acknowledged that, should he be writing an obit about her, he'd include one telling euphemism (as he and his colleagues do to entertain themselves from time to time): "disarming." It proves to be the one moment where their shared intimacy gives way to an honest truth she nevertheless rebukes ("That's not a euphemism!"). By film's end, when we learn that much of what Alice had told us was a constructed version of the truth (her real name is Jane Jones; she'd nicked Alice Ayres from a plaque at Postman's Park, rooting her entire life with Dan in a fanciful lie), it's clear that to know and therefore to love someone may not be the same thing. "What would falling in love look like if knowledge of oneself or another, of oneself as another, was not the aim or the result?" Phillips wonders, trying to establish flirting as a different mode of relating. "What would we be doing together if we were not getting to know each other? Another way of saying this might be to imagine a meeting or a relationship without (answerable) questions."

Closer flirts with those very questions. It's no surprise to find that the most honest conversation staged in the entire film happens in a private room at a strip club. It's there that, asked to tell Larry the truth, Alice offers up the following kernel of wisdom: "Lying is the most fun a girl can have without taking her clothes off. But it's better if you do," before being the most forthcoming she'll ever be. When asked for her name, she tells Larry she's named "plain Jane

Jones," which sounds like a lie but is, in fact, the truth. Larry thinks he knows Alice but he's also been made privy to the version of Alice (and Jane) she saw fit to put on for him. The irony is that she's most honest with him when she treats him like a stranger, refusing his insistent pleas to remember him from a few months back when they first met at Anna's gallery opening.

A stranger can offer us the chance to see ourselves anew. To imagine a different way of moving through the world. Every chance encounter, I've come to find, can be a chance to remake yourself. The unguarded intimacy that's nurtured in moments when we meet strangers we're enthralled with offers infinite possibilities to be better versions of ourselves. But also, maybe, to be and project the person we've always known ourselves to be. I'm reminded of T. S. Eliot's "The Love Song of J. Alfred Prufrock": "There will be time, there will be time," the poet writes in that seminal modernist piece, "To prepare a face to meet the faces that you meet." Meeting a new face is the perfect opportunity to prepare a new one for yourself. This is the very idea that opens another Mike Nichols piece, the 1971 battle-of-the-sexes drama *Carnal Knowledge*. "Everybody puts on an act," Susan (Candace Bergen) tells the awkward young man (Art Garfunkel's Sandy) who's hitting on her at a campus mixer. "So even if you meet someone," Sandy adds, hoping to show how much he agrees with her, "you don't know who you're meeting." All you're meeting is the act, not the person. Except Susan isn't ready to go that far. In fact, she objects to such a simplified version of what she's saying. "I think people only like to think they're putting on an act but it's not an act, it's really them. If they think it's an act they feel better because they think they can always change it," she tells Sandy. "It's an act. But they're the act. The act is them." All we have are our performances. Our masks. Our faces we put on to meet the faces we will meet. Are we, then, most ourselves when we meet a stranger? When such a performance feels, to the other, indistinguishable from the real thing? When said distinction is immaterial at best and insignificant at worst?

Ever since I heard Natalie Portman utter those two entrancing words, "Hello, stranger," I've been thinking about what such a greeting can mean—for myself. But also for larger meditations on how we relate to those closest to us, and how familiarity can breed a contentment that doesn't will away masks but calcifies them instead. Strangers, in this view, can be an escape. They can be a chance to rethink one's worldview (or to forget about the world altogether, however briefly). But they can also be thorns in the comfort of the life you've built, reminders of the many possibilities you have swatted away in the process. To flirt with a stranger is to flirt with infinite alternatives. In this sense, I am squarely in Phillips's camp: "Flirting may not be a poor way of doing something better," he writes, "but a different way of doing something else."

A stranger is always a (if not *the*) beginning. Or, even when it's not a beginning, it is an opening. So hello, stranger, and welcome to this journey where I will be unpacking my obsession with the fraught and fractious intimacies we build with those closest to us and, in the process, discover new ways of redrawing how we conceive *of* closeness. And learn, perhaps, how to flirt with the idea that estrangement (no matter how ephemeral) is a valid mode of sociability. A chance, even, to dream up new and more exciting ways of relating to others and, more crucially, to ourselves.

2.

MEET-CUTE

THERE'S A MOMENT. THERE'S ALWAYS A MOMENT.

You lock eyes with someone you've just met—or, more likely, someone you'd like to meet—and you just know. Or you tell yourself that you know. You want this moment, this very exchange, to mean something. To be the beginning of a storied romance that will become such when you tell the tale over and over again. It's a moment of connection, yes. But mostly it's a moment of recognition. The French call it *coup de foudre*. It's a lightning bolt moment of lucidity when you experience that seemingly mythic instance of falling head over heels. See? Even the English language cannot help but reach for cartoonishly exaggerated expressions with which to describe what happens when you spot "the one" amid a crowd. When you are, if we are really to invoke Greco-Roman mythology, pierced by Cupid's arrow. To hear Mercutio tell it in Shakespeare's famed play, the young, lovestruck Romeo "is already dead, stabbed with a white wench's black eye, run through the ear with a love-song, the very pin of his heart cleft with the blind bow-boy's butt-shaft." There's a bodily reaction here, a feeling that your senses have failed you, and an attendant pain that doubles as proof that who you've just interacted with is worthy of your gaze, of your affection, of your obsession, even.

Much of this rhetoric relies on the idea that whoever you've encountered is your "better half." I will admit, though, that the saying in Spanish is much more delectable: *media naranja* suggests you're one half of an orange who has suddenly found its missing half. It's a juicier concept, more viscerally connecting attraction with hunger, with thirst, with the sweetly acidic possibilities of coupledom. No matter what expression you choose, such a Platonic idea of romance and lovers has plenty of contemporary cultural currency. Look no further than John Cameron Mitchell's raucous punk rock musical *Hedwig and the Angry Inch*, which finds time, in between telling a story of an internationally ignored rock singer, to recount, in the song "The Origin of Love," the fable espoused by Aristophanes in Plato's *Symposium*. To find a beloved is to find someone who makes you whole; and in Hedwig's (and Aristophanes's) view, this is not merely a metaphor but a mythic truism. We've all been cleaved in half by Zeus, and so when we find our soulmate (yet another self-evident way in which we discuss the person we love), we're finding the person we once were separated from. Those moments of love at first sight are, if we follow this logic, a moment not only of recognition but of reunion. They come, also, from a scarcity mindset: once you encounter someone who so takes your breath away, you're inclined (encouraged, even!) to pursue them because you may never encounter them (or anyone like them) ever again.

Having grown up on a steady diet of telenovelas and rom-coms, I used to daydream about stringing out a love story from the briefest of moments. Ill equipped to imagine any other use for such meetings, I became a lovesick kid who put perhaps too much stock in those movie-ready moments, like when I first met my college boyfriend at a campus mixer, where our eyes did meet across a crowded room. Or when, in New York City years later, I was struck dumb when I clocked a cute, bespectacled boy on the dance floor staring at me. In all fairness, I may have also been staring at his imposing chest, which I then got to feel heaving against my own as we writhed to the sounds of late 2000s pop music, our bodies encouraged to think of each other as halves who'd found their perfect match amid a sea of other sweat-filled, grinding men. Intoxicated by the very scene swirling around me—disco balls, go-go dancers, salt-tinged kisses, and many a watered-down drink at this Chelsea bar—I didn't even hesitate to go home with him (to another borough via ferry at that!) nor to move in with him but months later (to Manhattan at least). All around me I was nudged to give outsize influence to moments like these: a bar hookup was the start of a story, not a narrative in itself. I was never able to simply enjoy those fleeting intimacies where I felt like I'd found someone unlike any other, someone who'd take my breath away like no one else could. When it came to romantic love, it seems, I was always reading for the plot, urging myself to narrativize any kind of intimate encounter with a stranger lest I lose my chance to proclaim I'd found my *media naranja*, no matter how sour that half soon turned out to be.

It's hard to stage any kind of talk of contemporary romance without engaging head-on with this kind of rhetoric. Such lovestruck infatuations remain central to the way we package, consume, and perpetuate romantic tales. In her poem titled "Love at First Sight," Nobel laureate Wisława Szymborska talks about the sudden passion that joins two lovers before reminding her readers that every beginning is only ever a sequel that is our life. Her turn toward narrative, toward seeing moments as beginnings—even to see our lives as a book of events—is a reminder that we apprehend what we experience, sometimes almost exclusively, in narratological terms. Literature, of course, is full of memorable instances of "love at first sight." But I am most partial to the one Patricia Highsmith stages in her 1952 novel, *The Price of Salt*. A now queer classic (further cemented as such with its 2015 big-screen adaptation, *Carol*), Highsmith's boundary-breaking and achingly touching romance begins in the unlikeliest of places: a department store. Therese, a shy shopgirl, is going about her day during the run-up to Christmas. She's come back from the employee break room, where she's had to use the cotton of a sanitary napkin to help stop the bleeding from her leg from a minor shopping-cart-related injury. Preoccupied with how much blood may still be running down her stocking, Therese finds herself back at the counter when it happens, the moment that will thenceforth change her life: "Their eyes met at the same instant," Highsmith writes. "Therese, glancing up from a box she was opening, and the woman just turning her head so she looked directly at Therese. She was tall and fair, her long figure graceful in the loose fur coat she held open with a hand on her waist. Her eyes were gray, colorless, yet dominant as light or fire, and caught by them, Therese could not look away."

Here is what Roland Barthes refers to as *ravissement*. In *A Lover's Discourse: Fragments*, a probing structural examination of the various "figures" in any love story (and therefore all love stories), the lauded queer critic reminds his reader that what we normally dub "love at first sight" (and what scholars label *enamoration*) is "the supposedly initial episode (though it may be reconstructed after the fact) during which the amorous subject is 'ravished' (captured and enchanted) by the image of the loved object." Therese is ravished. She experiences a moment frozen in time where she's struck dumb by the mere presence of a tall woman in a fur coat. What follows is that moment stretched through several pages during which Therese's own body seems to get away from her. She's flushed when the shopper approaches to ask her a question about a possible purchase and finds herself painstakingly examining the woman's eyebrows, her mouth, her eyes, and even her voice (which was "like her coat, rich and supple, and somehow full of secrets").

As she does her due diligence in helping Mrs. H. F. Aird with her shopping, Therese imagines a much more dramatic meeting. She wishes Mrs. Aird were more forward: "Are you really so glad to have met me?" she wishes Mrs. Aird would say. "Then why can't we see each other again? Why can't we even have lunch together today?" She says no such things. But she could have. Which is key to how Therese apprehends this moment and the ones that follow when she worries she'll have nothing else but these made-up possibilities. Therese "was conscious of the moments passing like irrevocable time, irrevocable happiness," Highsmith tells us, "for in these last seconds, she might turn and see the face she would never see again." What these possibilities open for Therese are also what's so central about those "love at first sight" moments: they allow us to imagine ourselves away from our everyday lives. They become imaginative leaps. They're rooted in this idea that to project oneself into a future with another—with a stranger, at that—requires assessing the kind of person you are and could still be. The push toward such a narrative impulse is one rooted in a sense of change, a sense of possibility, a sense that there is something about you you may wish to leave behind. But also, crucially, that there is something within you that will propel another one toward you.

Who among us hasn't been Therese, afraid that the striking stranger you just struck up a conversation with may just vanish forever, before you even get a chance to imagine a whole life (or maybe just a lunch date) with them? In that moment, Therese sees herself escaping the life she's known. Of course, the woman (Carol, we soon learn she's called) does reverse course and opens up a fissure in Therese's world, kindling a longing the shy shopgirl had long suppressed within herself. In Todd Haynes's film adaptation, the meeting between Therese and Carol isn't the first time we see the two women on-screen together. Haynes makes their interaction at the department store a flashback, both an explanation and an origin story for the intimacy we first witness between Cate Blanchett's titular character and Rooney Mara's shopgirl. In the opening moments of *Carol*, we see the two women seated for dinner, enjoying each other's company, until they're interrupted by a young man who inadvertently cuts short their evening together, egging Therese to leave Carol behind and join him at a party. En route to said party, looking out the window of the car taking her toward the life she's desperate to escape, Therese reminisces about the first time she laid eyes on Carol. True to Highsmith's prose, Haynes and screenwriter Phyllis Nagy make the most out of that chance Christmastime meeting. Only we're not made privy to Therese's many inner aches and inklings. Instead we're left with Mara's wordless awe when in the presence of Blanchett's fur-coated, well-poised customer. And it's a testament to both actresses that viewers understand the enormity of what goes on in what is otherwise a rather mundane interaction.

Then again, narratives about love at first sight depend on such mundanity. They happen at department stores because it's in those spaces where commingling of strangers is most obvious, most expected. You don't fall instantly for someone you've known for a while. Or work with. Or grew up with. You fall head over heels for someone when they enter your orbit as if flung from outer space. Maybe, as in *Closer*, when they get run over right across from you or when they're photographing you for your headshot. In romantic comedies, this is the moment where all stands still and our protagonist's life gets neatly directed toward a lovestruck narrative, sometimes even despite their protestations. One minute they're playing golf, say, and the next minute, as it happens in *Bringing Up Baby*, Cary Grant's tightly wound David Huxley finds himself unable to escape the gravitational pull of Katharine Hepburn's wily Susan Vance. In a way, that now classic 1938 flick has served as a template for this most formulaic of movie genres precisely because it hits its tropes with such abandon. In particular, the film's premise relied on the rom-com's most enduring conceit: the "meet-cute."

Bringing Up Baby could best be described as a series of meet-cutes, of moments when David and Susan crash into each other's lives. Following a mix-up at the golf course where her insouciance leaves him at a loss for words when she inadvertently steals and plays with his golf ball, the two keep meeting in somewhat random situations that bring them ever closer together. Susan ends up taking his car by mistake (again), leaving David agog at her total obliviousness to his own protestations. "You mean *this* is your car? *Your* golf ball? *Your* car? Is there anything in the world that doesn't belong to you?" she chides him, only to have him fire back the line the entire film will playfully bully him into retracting: "Yes, thank heaven, YOU!" Later, they meet again at a restaurant, where a rogue olive has David fall on his ass right in front of her, an incident that soon finds her ripping his waistcoat and he ripping her dress. The more he realizes the chaos she ushers in wherever she goes and the more he tries to avoid getting caught up in her outrageous shenanigans (which do end up involving a leopard called Baby), the more David is destined to never quite leave her side—throwing a previous engagement out the window by the time the credits roll. As he puts it toward the end of the film, "It isn't that I don't like you, Susan, because, after all, in moments of quiet, I'm strangely drawn toward you, but—well, there haven't been any quiet moments." Theirs is not a story of love at first sight. But it is one about how an indelible impression, no matter how grounded in screwball comedy it may be, sets up the romance between two unsuspecting strangers. In continually staging meet-cutes (at golf courses, in parking lots, at ritzy restaurants), *Bringing Up Baby* stands as a prime example of how the romantic comedy worked to reframe romance in decidedly modern terms, bringing down those mythic notions of "love at first sight" into more mundane territory.

The meet-cute is a prime example of the way Hollywood bastardized real-life emotions into unrealistic ready-made story templates. Jerrold Beim's aptly titled syndicated short story "They Met Cute," published in various newspapers in December 1945, offered what may well be the earliest and most lucid example of how studio moguls understood that now much-imitated rom-com trope. Beim's two-page tale was structured around the meeting between a Hollywood neophyte and a seasoned screenwriter: H. Tarrington Travis, "one of the greatest living novelists," has been tasked with working on a treatment of his novel with Bill Bailey, one of the studio's "Old Reliables" who knew how these highbrow literary types struggled when forced to write for the screen. The story opens with Bill bluntly telling H. T. that the way he'd just described a meeting of the film's protagonists could never work: "This is a motion picture," he tells him. "They've got to meet—cute." The short story ends up being a metafictional meditation on such meetings when, as Bill walks outside while trying to find a fun new way for his characters to be introduced to each other, he is struck (literally!) by a beautiful girl riding her bicycle. "This is wonderful—this is cute!" he tells her as she helps him up on his feet. Only, as he finds out soon after he invites her out on a date, the two *hadn't* just met; they were neighbors while growing up and were, in the words of her aunt, "old friends." And not, as Bill had hoped, new acquaintances. The ironic twist of those final lines stresses how implausible meet-cutes were. Meet-cutes didn't—couldn't—happen in real life. They were a fanciful fictional creation that was necessarily preposterous. And for that all the more aspirational. The sustained introspection of an omniscient narrator, as in Highsmith's novel, or that of a fellow character, as in Mercutio's dialogue, stretches out the time and the timing of such meetings, not to mention our own comprehension of them. The immediacy is made elastic, recursive even. The meet-cute demarcates a fictional, evanescing space. You can't remain there.

What feels preordained (or is rewritten as such in hindsight) is that those "love at first sight" moments become, in this more modern trope, a more expansive horizon. When we daydream of meet-cutes, of instances where we could fall in love at first sight with that stranger who's thrust upon us, what we're wishing is to collapse time: we encourage ourselves to go straight from a mere glance to a comforting intimacy. As if we were eager to skip key parts of the plot to get to the ending we're all supposed to aspire to.

The meet-cute is a passing moment. It's a narrative stepping stone that will necessarily get folded into a longer if rather formulaic rom-com narrative, the way Barthes suggests "love at first sight" scenes forever get constructed only in retrospect, always already having been turned into the beginning of a story. What to make, then, of narratives that seemingly do away with such a call? What could we envision if we remained in the meet-cute? If we didn't let go of the many possibilities inherent in such meetings? If we let ourselves inhabit that moment of longing where everything and perhaps nothing is possible? If we stretched it past its breaking point and lived in the uncertainty it so depends on? We may find a way to rewrite how it is we write and write about romantic stories. We may even find new ways of writing about the very concept of love altogether.

The ultimate template for such an effort remains, all these

decades later, Richard Linklater's *Before Sunrise*. One of the most romantic films from the nineties and brimming with Gen X sensibilities, Linklater's 1995 film demands to be read as equally a melancholy and cynical riff on the rom-com. Maybe this love story in miniature taking place over the course of one long evening (hence the title), should be better understood as a stretched-out moment: a feature-length meet-cute.

Despite the urgency its title suggests, *Before Sunrise* begins, instead, with a probing meditation on longevity. We're in a train car in Europe (en route to Paris, as it happens) and a couple is bickering in German. There's a rehearsed and resigned performativity to their arguing. They've been doing this (the traveling, the fighting) for a long time now. The man and woman may be exasperated but they're also quite at ease with said exasperation. Their unintelligible back-and-forth (for us non–German speakers) allows Jesse (Ethan Hawke), unable to concentrate on his book, to turn to Céline (Julie Delpy), who's equally annoyed by the car's distractions: "Do you have any idea what they were arguing about?" he asks her. She doesn't, alas, but takes the opportunity to offer Jesse, and the audience, a factoid that feels like a key to the film's themes: Did he know that as they grow older, men and women lose different kinds of hearing (men lose high-pitched sounds, women lower ones)? "Must be nature's way of allowing couples to grow old together and not kill each other," Jesse muses, almost to himself. Meant as an icebreaker between these two strangers, this opening conversation speaks to entrenched ideas about the pitfalls of long-term commitment. Pop culture, in fact, is awash with jokes about the inevitable way in which a couple will sour on each other as years and decades go by. Passion fades. Bitterness sets in. All that's left are cold comforts. Which are comforts, no doubt, but stripped of the fiery passion that once fueled them. In contrast to the German couple are Jesse and Céline, whose playful banter soon leads to flirtation, and then, when the two get off in Vienna (she forgoing her Paris destination to share one night with Jesse), into a strange familiarity made all the more appealing by its own transience. They will only have one night. There'll be no years and decades ahead during which they'll see themselves grateful to be losing their hearing lest they have to endure one another's petty annoyances.

It's hard not to read (despite its romantic trappings) a kind of wearied knowingness to the film's own strict structuring device. How much of the buoyant flirtation that takes place between Jesse and Céline is helped, in no small part, by the fact that they know they only have this one night together? One that, they insist, they don't want spoiled with any thought to a possible future—let alone any kind of sexual intimacy? Theirs is a love story precisely because it is only about a passing moment. Presciently, the film's poster asked audiences point-blank whether the greatest romance of your life could last only one night (yes, we're encouraged to answer). As critic Dennis Lim writes regarding Linklater's trilogy, "The shifting meaning of a moment—as it is anticipated and then experienced, as it is remembered or misremembered, as it gains or loses luster in a year, a decade, or more—is the existential question that animates the story of Jesse and Céline."

One of the joys of *Before Sunrise*, even with its schematic and rigidly gendered dichotomies (American/European, dreamer/realist, etc.) is its aimlessness. Linklater and his cowriter, Kim Krizan, wrote what amounts to plotless film. Such a drifting sense of direction actually made the film (per its poster) all the more romantic. This is a movie all about possible beginnings. And about endless possible endings. About the very fleeting intimacies we can let ourselves carve out with others when we let our guard down and allow them in in ways that sound (and feel and look!) crazy.

To tell a contemporary—a nineties!—love story required disassembling the very structure *of* a love story. And it's a call to question how inherited "romantic" ideals are as stifling as they are illusory—what Jesse calls everyone's "romantic projections." During one of their many debates on the nature of relationships, the two seem to agree that there is no such thing as a happy couple. Or, if there is, it's one rooted in lies. In the film, their back-and-forth about the challenges of married couples—which includes Céline sharing how her grandmother had kept a long-lost love a secret from her husband for decades—is cut short by Jesse's playfulness. When called out for being a sappy romantic, he teases and tickles Céline before Linklater cuts to them picking up their conversation at an outdoor café a while later.

In the original script, though, Jesse went even further with his faux cynicism: "That's the thing about relationships," he says. "People are always saying, 'I want to know you, I want to know who you are.' But it is so hard for anyone to even know themselves. Who I am is always changing, so how can anyone else share in that?" The seemingly existential question Jesse poses to himself nevertheless captures the sentiments he comes to embody throughout the finished cut of the film. What he's espousing is this notion that to fall for someone requires knowledge. Seduction is a kind of epistemology. You're encouraged to know more about your beloved in order to love them more, and to lure your way into their life. The tension of *Before Sunrise* is whether such a happenstance meeting is made to feel all the more powerful because of its contingency: they only have a few hours, after all. The two opt to make the most of them. And so, Jesse and Céline spend much of the film ostensibly getting to know each other (finding things both charming and off-putting in each other's personalities), all the while wondering aloud whether the kind of extended flirtation they're engaged in is at all sustainable. More pointedly, they allow themselves to enjoy their night together precisely because they will never get to truly know one another. They are and will remain strangers even when, at the end of their night together, they promise to meet again in six months' time.

Time is the main antagonist of the film. Not just because the time Jesse and Céline have is limited but because everywhere they turn (and every conversation they have) hints at the dooming powers of time. It's why Jesse quotes W. H. Auden's poem "As I Walked Out One Evening," using its wholly romantic rhythms to good use in further seducing Céline. Published in 1940's *Another Time* collection, the piece stages a debate between a young naive lover who believes "Love has no ending" and the clocks in the city that insist "You cannot conquer Time." The question is whether love can endure. Not whether love can be eternal but whether it can weather the unending pressures of the tyrannical clock, the unending days that crash into and onto your idyllic infatuation. Like Auden's other most lauded poem from that same collection, "Funeral Blues" (popularized after its inclusion in a key scene in *Four Weddings and a Funeral*, the English poet clearly hitting a chord in the mid-nineties), "As I Walked Out One Evening" is preoccupied with how to comprehend a concept as illusory as Time itself. Not just in the way we approach our own mortality—though there was that, given how World War II was creeping into the poet's own daily worries—but in the way it helps structure our own lives. "Life leaks away," as Jesse quotes Auden saying. It gets in the way of the romance, of that undying love the dreamer and dreamy lover envisions.

Before Sunrise invokes Auden when our pair see their time together vanishing right before their eyes—and forces them, in the process, to break the promise they'd made each other (and, perhaps, dooming the kind of future they might have had without the other, but let's leave that to *Before Sunset* and *Before Midnight*, shall we?). To think the two could've actually stopped time if they'd opted to leave their fanciful flirtation as the brief thing it was always designed to be. For what better way to fool time and the narratives of romantic ideals it depends on than by embracing the transitory and refusing the call to move forward at all?

At the end of *Before Sunrise*, Jesse and Céline come to acknowledge that they want to dispense with the rules they'd set for themselves. They run up against the imperative of any two strangers who find themselves enthralled with each other. They see in each other a mirror they wish to cling to, an idea they hope to further explore. For that is what every meet-cute leads to: a new reality, a new world order, even if only at the emotional level. Therein lies the romantic thrust of the film: you want the two to commit to their future meeting. Except, why should they? Why can't they just embrace the passing nature of their encounter? Why do we not make room for such fleeting intimacies? Why must we adhere to the tyranny of romantic commitment?

Before Sunrise, of course, sketches out this very tension. The reason Jesse and Céline won't allow their dreamy one-night stand of sorts to remain as such is because the rhetoric of romance (like the kind found, say, in Auden's poetry) does not value those types of interactions. What's worthy is what lasts. What endures. What's here today and gone tomorrow is to be mourned, not treasured— even when there's ample evidence that what erodes is just as valued and valuable in our everyday lives. Here's why Auden ends up serving as a perfect metatext for Linklater and his characters. The poet's heartrending works have, for decades now, lived side by side with his own tumultuous romantic relationship with his longtime lover, Chester Kallman, a man whom Auden couldn't live without and who'd arrived in his life as if thrust from outer space, affirming the very way he'd envisioned falling in love but a year prior. In a poem titled "O Tell Me the Truth About Love," Auden had wondered how love would find him: "When it comes," the last stanza opens, "will it come without warning, / Just as I'm picking my nose?" Love would find him, he imagines, amid the everyday. The poem focuses on how love is enshrined as the thing that is all but waiting for you just around the corner. "Will it alter my life altogether?" he asks a few lines after. Meeting Kallman had done that, to the point where Auden dedicated *Another Time* to him, penning a beautifully romantic poem in the acknowledgments that nevertheless opens and closes with a rather dour line ("Every eye must weep alone"). But the poet spent much of his later years coming to the realization that the romantic ideals he had for companionship with Kallman were not to be; Kallman insisted on living a sexual life outside their decades-long companionship, which strained their own.

Dorothy J. Farnan, Kallman's stepmother, noted that the two men clashed at an almost fundamental level about how to prize the intimacies they demanded of each other. In fact, speaking about her own experience with Chester's father, Farnan writes that when a Kallman man fell in love "it was always for the first time." She implies that Chester, like his father, liked the beginning of things, the thrill of a meeting, of a flirtation, and enjoyed privileging that over the sustained work of long-standing companionship. "The only trouble was that the love seldom lasted," she adds. "They needed the challenge of other hearts. As time went by, you realized that you could be just so close and no closer; yet you wanted to possess this man as he possessed you, for he was the best of lovers, and you knew that you would never again meet anyone who could take his place." This is what makes a film like *Before Sunrise* feel heartrendingly romantic. Focused on that first time—on that meet-cute—it cannot offer anything but a flashing snapshot of the relationship that could be. It's all in the promise of a future, not the aching pains of the present. In quoting Auden, Linklater's film makes us wonder whether something premised on its own ephemerality can be made to endure.

Close to three decades after *Before Sunrise* first wormed its way into our hearts, a budding canon of queer films has taken up its narrative conceit and pushed it to the center of LGBTQ stories about romance. For a community that has long needed to depend on passing connections and fragile makeshift intimacies (in bars, in alleys, in chat rooms, on marches), the *Before Sunrise* template feels all the richer. It's offered contemporary filmmakers the chance to enshrine encounters that have, for decades (if not longer), been central to how so many of us explore our own desires—in transient spaces and fleeting meetings we sometimes don't allow to (or often can't let) exist once the sun comes up.

Jacques Martineau and Olivier Ducastel's 2016 erotic drama *Paris 05:59: Théo & Hugo*, for instance, stages a luminous meet-cute at a Parisian sex club and invites us to follow its titular characters as they bike and bond with each other after their steamy hookup amid writhing and sweaty bodies—all before their sexual intimacy (read: their barebacking encounter) upends their closeness once the specter of an HIV transmission redraws the night they hoped to have had. More recently, Goran Stolevski's wistful Australia-set 2022 film *Of an Age* captures the yearning that can be fostered with one chance encounter between two men on one pivotal day in their youth, which will bond them irrevocably for decades after. But the most salient example remains Andrew Haigh's touching 2011 film *Weekend*, where a one-night stand between Glen (Chris New), a jaded militant queer, and Russell (Tom Cullen), a bashfully romantic closeted bloke, gives way to bruising conversations about intimacy between gay men in the twenty-first century. Glen, like *Sex, Lies, and Videotape*'s Graham before him, has turned taped discussions with the men he's slept with into fodder for a still-shapeless art project: he enjoys picking apart the way those first sexual experiences with a stranger set us up to think of ourselves as blank canvases ready to be sketched on by such intimate moments. But Haigh's film, like Linklater's, cannot escape the pull toward romance, toward narrative. Glen's project seems to melt away in the presence of charming Russell, who wishes (again, echoing Jesse and Céline) he were able to extend this pivotal weekend into something more. Into something longer. Into something that would and could endure.

My favorite of this avowedly limited canon of romantic films is Lucio Castro's *Fin de siglo* (*End of the Century*), a 2019 Spanish film that further upends the *Before Sunrise* template. The Barcelona-set film is both an ode to and a deconstruction of a thrilling one-night encounter (two of them, actually, twenty years apart). After eyeing each other at the beach, Ocho (Juan Barberini) invites Javi (Ramon Pujol) over to his apartment when he sees him walking below the balcony of his Airbnb. Their hookup leads to a long evening spent together, sharing some bread, cheese, and wine on a rooftop, all while sharing more about themselves and their lives. We learn Ocho has just broken up with his boyfriend of twenty years and that Javi has a daughter with his husband in Berlin. Their twinned visions of long-term intimacy are equally unsettling. Ocho admits his breakup was brought on by his desire to find himself anew and alone. Javi confesses he and his husband rarely have sex anymore (ergo their sexual openness).

It's only once they start probing further into what they do and who they are that Ocho says the words that turn *Fin de siglo* on its head: "Siento que te había conocido desde antes," he says. But it's not just an inkling. "Sí," Javi replies. They *have* met before. And so the movie flashes back twenty years to when a closeted Ocho arrives in Barcelona to stay at his friend Sonia's place. But when she leaves unexpectedly, he's left to sightsee the city with her then boyfriend: Javi. Castro doesn't de-age his actors. Nor does he attempt to visually distinguish them from their future counterparts. Actors Barberini and Pujol look exactly the same as they had minutes earlier as they wander through town walking, drinking, and eventually hooking up—a moment that soon rushes back to present-day Ocho, who feels foolish for not having recognized Javi right away, especially since he'd been wearing the Kiss shirt the two had grabbed when it had fallen on them in the middle of street from a stray clothesline all those years ago. There's a desire to disorient the viewer here. To collapse past and present. To equate the fleeting intimacy of a cruising encounter (of their queered meet-cute) with the familiar one the young men enjoyed all those years ago.

But Castro doesn't stop there. *Fin de siglo* folds into itself one more time. After Javi and Ocho are done reminiscing about their youthful encounter two decades prior and the former leaves to avoid further messiness with his husband back at home, Ocho turns from his Airbnb balcony back to his life. Only he stumbles on a child's toy. We enter, then, a different though entirely familiar space: the Barcelona apartment is the same but it is now inhabited by Javi, Ocho, and their daughter. That fridge we'd just seen be depressingly empty (it was an Airbnb after all) is now fully stocked with groceries for a family of three. Yet again Castro doesn't explain what is happening. Is this a different timeline? A "what if?" scenario playing out in Ocho's head? Could it be a dream? Gone is the pair's passionate desire for each other. Now they spend their nights reading in bed, or watching TV on their tablets, eventually (almost begrudgingly) agreeing to have sex. Later, Ocho tells Javi he just had a dream where he had a long-term boyfriend who wasn't Javi. And then, as if the spell had been broken once more, Javi exits the apartment, leaving Ocho at his balcony once again waving goodbye to a young handsome stranger in a Kiss shirt. Then and now collapse into each other. Such ephemeral closeness is nestled within long-term companionship. Why choose when you could imagine both simultaneously?

The now is the tense of the meet-cute. Of flirtation. Of possibility. A temporality divorced from commitment to a future, away from commitment itself. To remain in that space (in that time) seems futile but not, for that, any less entrancing. Jesse and Céline do not want to become that old German couple. Ocho and Javi would perhaps prefer to remain madly in lust with each other than to settle for the bland comforts of married life. Yet what's refreshing about *Fin de siglo* (especially compared to *Before Sunrise*, whose singularity has since been dashed by its sequels) is that those are not presented as mutually exclusive choices. Here are two men who are intimate strangers, whose intimacy, in fact, swings from familiarity to estrangement with a mere jump cut. If what Glen is so worried about in *Weekend* was finding his own sense of self rotted by and for the eyes of another ("I'm trying to redraw myself . . . but everyone keeps fucking hiding my pencil," he moans), *Fin de siglo* nudges us to imagine a different kind of narrative that would disallow such calcified artistic possibilities.

This is the queerest and most radical (re)vision of Linklater's premise yet. In form and content, Castro's film rewrites the rules of modern romance, disavowing old notions of how a story is supposed to begin, let alone end. And it finds its conceptual North Star in the unlikeliest of places: David Wojnarowicz's *Close to the Knives: A Memoir of Disintegration*. The American artist and photographer, best known for his queer militant sensibility and inflammatory artistry rooted in pushing against the very notions of normalcy (and progress and power and narrative, even), is singled out in a key moment in the film where his words quite literally take over the screen. The lines, presented as text laid over the image of Ocho reading them for the first time, make us acutely aware of their power. They serve as a promise for the film's own romantic ideals that we could all embrace more forcefully; they imagine a way out of the teleology of romance and dream up a theory of love and time that's rooted in the promising possibilities of what's fleeting, of what's possibly tenuous and, for that, conceptually powerful and resonant: "I'm getting closer to the coast and realize how much I hate arriving at a destination," Wojnarowicz writes. "Transition is always a relief. Destination means death to me. If I could figure out a way to remain forever in transition, in the disconnected and unfamiliar, I could remain in a state of perpetual freedom." Wojnarowicz's plea feels utopian because it's so unfeasible. Here is deferral not as avoidance but as an expansive possible, as a desirous horizon: a sense that it is only in movement that we can be most at peace. He urges us to want to spend our nights (in Prague, in London, in Barcelona) not worried about what's to come but excited about what's ahead. We'd look, then, not for endings (for destinations) but for journeys. And detours. And endless transitions where we could continually let ourselves be as free as could be.

3.

ON SEXTING

ANONYMITY MAKES EVERYONE A STRANGER.

This was the promise of the Y2K internet. Back then, those of us who had access to dial-up on our bulky desktops cherished the ability to surf the net with little worry that those we encountered in forums, chat rooms, and comments sections would know who we were. This was the equalizing premise of the World Wide Web. For queer kids like myself, the chance to have, as we were told, the world at our fingertips (imagine that!) meant we could move through spaces with a stealth that was as emboldening as it was necessary. Sure, I had to scrub browser histories at lightning speed if I hoped to keep certain online searches to myself. But whenever I was seated in front of a computer armed with an internet connection (no matter how shoddy, and boy, were some of them unbearably slow!), I felt like I could be whoever I wanted to be. I could push away the shy, bookish kid I was and pretend to be an older, wiser, and proudly out teenager who knew what the hell he was doing when he downloaded gay porn, scrolled through queer erotica, and cruised many an online chat room where other boys like me (and, no doubt, just as many men) were seeking similar thrills. The privacy of the internet helped me figure out who I was and who I could be. By being, however fleetingly, a stranger who was everything I could be and want in others.

I wasn't the only one who felt this way. On July 5, 1993, *The New Yorker* cartoonist Peter Steiner captured this very sentiment in a soon-to-be-iconic strip that became shorthand for the joy of net anonymity: "On the internet, nobody knows you're a dog." The accompanying picture? A gleeful dog at a keyboard relaying this truism to a fellow canine. The expansive possibilities of online self-fashioning (no one needed to know I was a horny high schooler searching AltaVista for frat boy porn) were thrilling. The imaginative leaps I could take when striking up a conversation with a(ny) guy online served me well. They were the first instances where I could take labels like *gay* and *queer* out for a drive in between slow-loading JPEGs and heavily pixelated MP4 downloads. Where I could let my lustful fantasies run wild with no worries about frightful health scares. Even the shame that very much drove me to these seemingly illicit (and yet so easily found) online spaces was quelled by the makeshift community I found there. I learned not only about what I wanted but what I could allow myself to crave. To be. To embody.

But such virtual forays left me adrift in the real world; screen names like XXXMan (I was nothing if not a horny nerd even in these fantasy worlds) left my teenage and then college self unable to suture those online cravings with intimate, in-person interactions. In fact, when "TheFacebook" arrived at the University of British Columbia while I was an undergrad there, I struggled with how to bridge the gap between my online persona and the public-facing one such online directories (and later social networks) would demand of me. Social media would come to encourage connections with strangers but only if you forsook the safety of anonymity the internet once afforded us. By 2015, Kaamran Hafeez would accurately update Steiner's early nineties formulation with his own twist: "Remember when, on the Internet, nobody knew who you were?" a rueful dog asks another, while their owner hunches over his home office computer. It took roughly two decades, but the advent of social media networks and the increased consolidation of tech giants meant that our privacy (our data, really, the two being one and the same in such spaces) would become a publicly traded commodity.

As I try to think back on all the sites I frequented in my late teens and early twenties, I realize how much harder it is nowadays to freely roam through spaces like those. Manroulette, for instance, which had begun as a gay spin-off of Chatroulette, a site where you could cycle through various folks broadcasting their not-safe-for-work exploits on cam, now requires a log-in if you want to activate your own webcam. This extra step kept me, I'll admit, from once again indulging in what was a regular pastime in my college years.

As a millennial (a geriatric one, so I'm told) whose formative years were punctuated by the increased reach and accessibility of online spaces, I can't ever look back on my own coming out (let alone my own coming-of-age) without examining the role the budding World Wide Web had on my sexual awakening and ensuing sexual education. I first learned how to flirt with a boy (or man, more likely) not in person but via text. I didn't first offer my naked body to a guy in the privacy of his bedroom but within the privacy of my desktop. Over the years, I've wondered what the inadvertent effects of such compartmentalization did to my (queer) sense of self. For decades, even while dating boys I was clearly infatuated with—in love with even, or so I insisted—I couldn't shake off the desire to flirt and cruise other boys (strangers, mostly) online while simultaneously understanding such an impulse as inherently shameful and best kept to myself. What was first a boon of privacy became shrouded, instead, in secrecy.

And so, rather than pursue what those titillating scenarios brought up for me, I opted instead to set my sights on the storybook romance I'd decided would and could finally be mine. The monogamous couple (its qualifier so often deployed by its absence) was a hermetically sealed intimacy I pursued with abandon in my twenties. This was the promise realized of coming out, finally. I could flirt with boys in person and imagine futures with them following campus meet-cutes. Which I did. The pull of my online cruising, of the incessant thrills sexting gave me, remained; only I boxed them away and pushed them far from the fabric of my real-life experience. Those days I found myself alone in my apartment, itching to get off and wanting to do so on cam for some stranger, or hoping to accomplish it after getting salacious texts and photos from thirsty online acquaintances, I would tell myself that what I was doing was harmless. It was all virtual and therefore all rather ephemeral. None of it had any tangible effects on my relationship, on my everyday life. I kept that all to myself, helped in no small part by the fact that I could, at any given moment, tune it all out with a simple swipe. It was all on my smartphone, after all; no longer did I need that clunky desktop from my youth. Nor the permanence of an Ethernet cable. My iPhone had made all those fantasies portable.

My phone, in fact, was the last vestige of privacy I had. Over the years, it had become the repository for all the things I wanted to keep hidden—from others and even from myself. Apps like Snapchat and Instagram, presumably created to help us connect with friends and strangers alike, became places where I leveraged public interactions into decidedly more intimate (more private, more secret) conversations, which in turn led to racier and much more volatile intimacies. I'd be lying if I said I didn't enjoy getting a cute guy to send me a dick pic precisely because it skirted the line of propriety. The furtiveness of it all added to its fun. It soon became a pastime. One I enjoyed and indulged in way too much. The fear of not wanting to get caught (by my boyfriend, later my husband) was assuaged by the deluded inner pep talks I gave myself. All of this was preferable to actually meeting up with guys or going cruising out in the streets, no?

There was vanity here. And some serious self-esteem issues. With some shame thrown in for good measure. Away from the prying eyes of those who knew me best (or thought they did; how scandalized would they have been to find out everything I did on camera for strangers who knew flattery would get them everywhere?) I could refashion myself as a confident flirter, a skilled cruiser who knew exactly what he wanted and who could get others to want him in ways he'd never have imagined possible. For sexting is an artform. Maybe this is the writer in me but I'm bullish enough to stand by such a statement. If you've ever spent time in an online forum or began a thirsty DM conversation with an online crush (an *oomf* in contemporary online queer lingo), you've probably come across folks who are utterly lousy at it. Sexting, after all, requires a curious blend of seriousness and playfulness. Of coyness and brazenness. Personally, I gravitate toward (and perform best) when I hit that sweet spot between sly and smutty. I like to ensnare boys into sharing more than they bargained for. I like to surprise them with thoughts and words and photos that thrill them precisely because they're unexpected. I love being told that I've taken the conversation too far, that they shouldn't have sent those nudes (even though it was fun), that they hope I understand (their boyfriend wouldn't).

But no matter how artful my theoretical acrobatics were when it came to maintaining those illicit interactions cordoned off from my (yes, monogamous) relationships—including, as it turns out, my marriage—I eventually had to contend with an undeniable truth: the most honest conversations about what I wanted and who I wanted to be, about what I desired and the desires I hoped to elicit, were happening outside the purview of what I construed as the most intimate relationship in my life. Such interactions didn't materially affect the intimacy I'd constructed with live-in partners, I told myself. Until they did, of course. For a stray nude and its attendant sexting is what proved to be the final nail in the coffin of my marriage: my phone eventually laid bare frustrations (sexual and otherwise) that had been simmering for close to a decade. This conundrum of mine is not unique to our current day and age. Stray letters and illicit exchanges have long felled relationships (originally, my undergraduate thesis was going to be all about *Les Liaisons dangereuses!*). But our technology has markedly changed how such intimacies are negotiated. And so, while the disastrous consequences of quite lecherous communications may be nothing new—as Pierre Choderlos de Laclos's epistolary novel deftly illustrates—its twenty-first-century trappings have truly complicated how we navigate them. Thankfully, it feels like pop culture is finally keeping apace with how these age-old questions are being reimagined in our smartphone age.

The title for Paolo Genovese's 2016 film *Perfetti sconosciuti* is an all-too-obvious nod to the idea that no matter how close you think you are with your partner, you may always remain "perfect strangers" to each other. Yet that translation loses a bit of the linguistic play at work in the Italian. *Sconosciuti*, like *desconocido* in Spanish, speaks just as much to strangeness and estrangement as it does to the unknown and the unknowable. The premise of Genovese's comedy rests on how (im)perfectly we let ourselves be known to those whom we are most familiar with. During a rare lunar eclipse, married couple Rocco and Eva (Marco Giallini and Kasia Smutniak) are hosting a dinner party for their friends. That includes Carlotta and Lele (Anna Foglietta and Valerio Mastandrea), whose own marriage seems to be at a standstill, made slightly worse by the fact that they live not just with their two young kids but with Lele's mother. They're joined as well by relative newlyweds Cosimo and Bianca (Edoardo Leo and Alba Rohrwacher), who brim with the first blush of passion their friends not-so-secretly covet. They're all to welcome another couple: Peppe (Giuseppe Battiston) is to bring his new girlfriend, Lucilla. Only, he shows up alone. He apologizes for her absence. She's sick, they're all told, and unhappy that she won't finally be able to meet Peppe's close-knit friend group that dates all the way back to their joyful school days.

As all the couples (and Peppe) organize themselves around the dinner table, it's obvious there are strains each of them are attempting to brush off, if only for the evening. Issues of parenting, sexual intimacy, and family planning are at the forefront of various conversations as these seven friends sit down and begin catching up with each other. In the middle of a conversation about what everyone shares with one another, and especially with one's romantic partners, Eva (a therapist) suggests a party game: What if, for the remainder of the meal, everyone seated agreed to be as transparent as possible? Would they all agree to keep their phones face up on the table and to read out any incoming message and answer every call on speakerphone? The awkward laughter and banter that follows speaks to the ludicrousness of such a request. Who could possibly agree to such a thing? Surely no one would be so cavalier about the privacy they've come to enjoy on their phones, right? But the game puts them all in a bind: you would only object to playing if you had something to hide. Refusing to participate would be the easiest way of admitting guilt. And so, implausibly, one by one the friends agree to play this dangerous social game.

At first it *is* all fun and games. When a befuddled Cosimo gets a message from an unknown number that reads "I want your body," the table readies itself for a juicy confrontation—one that's quickly punctured by Rocco revealing he'd sent the message himself from his teenage daughter's phone. Soon, though, the dinner party devolves into a frayed mind game where every message and call becomes a minefield to avoid if not outright disarm. Incessant phone calls from coworkers become indicative of an ongoing, adulterous relationship. Text messages from retirement homes (about possible openings) and medical facilities (for upcoming plastic surgery appointments) dredge up long-simmering resentments that are made all the worse by being aired out in front of such an unintended audience.

"Our phones are our black box," one character explains. They are where we store our darkest secrets. But they also end up serving as unvarnished documents of who we are and who we'd like to be. They're perhaps only made available to others once we're gone and our loved ones choose to figure out what led to such wreckage. Such insights into the role our phones play in our private sense of self-fashioning feels even truer close to a decade after Genovese's film first came out. That's because our lives have steadily been migrating online, with social media apps constantly nudging us to not merely project our day-to-day onto the internet for all to see (for likes and shares and follows; remember when we used lyrics in our MSN Messenger away messages, dutifully posted what we had for breakfast, and blissfully checked into whatever entertainment venue we were at on any given day?), but to forcibly understand our existence as constantly being filtered by the many ways in which we interact virtually with one another. Our smartphones constantly blur the line between public and private. What happens in your phone is (theoretically, terms and conditions aside) private.

Yet such privacy is paraded publicly, literally at times, as you can access quite private affairs in full view of the public, checking your email or your DMs in cars and subways, on sidewalks and in cafés, in offices and drive-throughs—but also in more abstract ways, as your online presence makes you a public-facing individual who doles out private moments through any given social media post. *Perfetti sconosciuti*'s premise preys on this very promise. Didactic though they may be, Genovese's characters play out a charade that feels depressingly familiar to many of us who have had to hopscotch our way around extramarital intimacies that were as threatening as they were thrilling.

On its surface, *Perfetti sconosciuti* tests the limits of privacy within a couple. When Eva learns that her husband has been secretly going to therapy for months, her ideas about how she felt Rocco undermined and dismissed her own profession come crashing down. But is that the same (whether in kind or in degree) as Bianca learning that Cosimo had just gotten another woman pregnant when the two were trying to start a family together? One is about privacy. The other about secrecy. The former feels necessary within any healthy relationship; the latter cannot help but chip away at the trust needed for a solid foundation. But both seem like sides of the same coin: intimacy, after all, exists at the intersection between privacy and secrecy. When we're intimate with someone else, we invite them into our own private space (into our private sense of self, even)—and that can involve letting someone in on what would otherwise remain secret in more public environments.

Intimate is both an adjective and a verb. You intimate that which is yours alone to share, to those you wish to be intimate with. "To intimate," as queer theorist Lauren Berlant argues, "is to communicate with the sparest of signs and gestures, and at its root intimacy has the quality of eloquence and brevity." It's a language as well, one you build and tinker with over time. Inside jokes and knowing gazes help bolster those very intimacies, making us feel like we're building something together—a couple, a home, a family. I also mean *build* in a more literal (though, of course, more figurative) sense: intimacy is an emotional architecture whose designs help delineate the public and the private. What's allowed within it is as important as what's left outside. When you grow close to someone, you invite them into your privacy. You envelop them in your private world. You welcome them into your private spaces—into your very own notion *of* privacy. The bedroom, if we want to be literal, yes. But the bathroom and the closet as well. You welcome them into your innermost expressions of what's private, what's intimate.

"But intimacy also involves an aspiration for a narrative about something shared," Berlant adds, "a story about both oneself and others that will turn out in a particular way." These stories we know by heart. They are familiar because of their ubiquity. Think of the couple. Think of marriage. Think of the family. These are intimacies that are socially sanctioned and encouraged. They allow the intimate to become public by its very appeal to privacy. Berlant connects those narratives to "institutions of intimacy" that are designed (or hope) to be both beautiful and long lasting. The married couple is its most obvious example: the intimacy between spouses is not only socially sanctioned but perfectly legible. Theirs is a closeness that everything from the law to religion—and yes, even popular culture—exalts and understands. *Perfetti sconosciuti* stages an all-out assault on such an institution by forcing its many married couples to grapple with the shortcomings their shared intimacies have helped erupt. In each case, their intimacies have been breached in all-too-familiar ways.

Since its arrival on Italian screens in 2016, Genovese's film has become a global phenomenon. With over twenty adaptations all over the world (including in Israel, Iceland, Spain, Mexico, and Japan), *Perfetti sconosciuti* currently holds the Guinness World Record as the most remade movie in history. Such reach is a testament to its universal appeal. Here is a decidedly modern provocation; it's actually quite refreshing to watch a romantic dramedy capture the seductive power of sending and receiving nudes—especially without your partner's consent. That's the bind Carlotta and Lele find themselves in when we learn both had been enjoying such extramarital extracurriculars: she taking photos for a Facebook friend she's never met in real life, he receiving them from a flirty stranger who gets off on showing off. Such revelations disrupt what seemed already, to friends and audiences, like a marriage at a crossroads. There's a beautiful symmetry at work here. Both halves of the couple crossed lines they knew they shouldn't have. But there's a blindness to what they were doing. Aware they were not getting the attention (sexual and otherwise) from each other, they sought it from somewhere else. But unlike Cosimo and Eva, who were secretly seeing each other behind their partners' backs, the photos Carlotta and Lele exchanged left them feeling like they weren't (not *really*) materially affecting their own marriage. Genovese does a great job in fleshing out that seemingly impossible argument—especially because it sounds outrageous only when it's used as an excuse.

I first chanced upon this Italian film through its Mexican adaptation. Manolo Caro, who'd done wonders queering the telenovela with his outlandish Netflix series *La Casa de las Flores*, took on *Perfectos desconocidos* back in 2018 and gamely treated his straight characters with the requisite flippant humor Genovese had flirted with. When Pepe (Franky Martín) arrives without Lucía in tow, the women around him can't help but badger him into telling them all about her. Could he really be in love? If he spends thirty minutes talking about her, says Ana (Ana Claudia Talancón), he's definitely in love. He bashfully asks what it means if it's more like seventy minutes: he's madly in love, Flora (Mariana Treviño) concedes. It's then that the punch line of the back-and-forth arrives: if he doesn't talk about her at all, it means they're married. That's uttered by the Lele character, Ernesto (Miguel Rodarte), who immediately gets scoffed at by his wife, Flora. The exchange is slightly different in Italian: in Genovese's original film, the friends don't measure love in how many minutes a couple spends talking about each other but in those they spend talking *to* each other. Communication, in either formulation, blooms when love is new and craters when it's sanctified by marriage. Lele/Ernesto's immature joke undergirds the central thesis of every single iteration of *Perfect Strangers*: whatever stirring intimacies you have with strangers, those who don't yet know you well, will disappear in time when they finally become intimate partners.

The film's themes about the secrets we keep from others, and from ourselves, know no borders. They speak just as easily to Italians and Russians as to Indonesians and South Koreans. This feels both disheartening and understandable. Especially because the most devastating "secret" disclosed throughout the night—the one made to stand alongside and therefore akin to flagrant affairs and petty marital lies—is Pepe's homosexuality. You see, there is no "Lucilla" to be met. There *is* a Lucio, though. Despite how close he feels to his friends, this nebbish-looking teacher (who, it turns out, was fired for coming out) does not trust that he'd find a wholly supportive environment if he were to be honest about who he really is and who he's now dating. His fear turns out to be well founded. His male friends do not take well to the idea that one of them could be gay—and has been all of this time. More to the point, they struggle with the notion that one of their own could have kept something so central to his identity from them all for so many years. Ironic, not to mention hypocritical, given the way so many of them keep secrets of their own from friends and wives alike.

Secrets, of course, especially during such fraught moonlit evenings as the one captured in *Perfetti sconosciuti*, have a way of creeping out. Just ask the group of gay friends that make up Mart Crowley's 1968 play *The Boys in the Band*, arguably the most obvious example of what happens when a party game gets dangerously out of hand. Crowley's play is set during one fateful night when a birthday celebration becomes an embittered battle of the wills as those there gathered are enticed to take part in the most cruel late-night game the American stage had seen since Edward Albee's deluded married couple in his play *Who's Afraid of Virginia Woolf?* had traumatized their guests with their brutal "Humiliate the Host" but a few years prior. Gathered for their friend Harold's birthday, a group of gay male friends in New York City in the late 1960s (pre-Stonewall, if we must be accurate, though William Friedkin's film adaptation came out months after those fateful 1969 summer riots) opt to, at their host Michael's urging, play a game called "Affairs of the Heart." As Michael explains it, their evening's entertainment "is a combination of both the Truth Game and Murder—with a new twist." There's only one rule: you must call on the telephone the one person "we truly believe we have loved."

The phone, yet again, serves as the fulcrum through which connection and (self-)isolation, honesty and (self-)deception will be made visible as private conversations and (self-)disclosures are made public. Seems simple enough. Though, as it becomes clear during the play's second act, Michael's made-up pastime has been designed to open old wounds and perhaps cut up a few new ones in the process. The real aim of this telephonic charade is Alan. A college friend of Michael's who may or may not be on the verge of a revealing disclosure (he'd called Michael earlier in the evening in tears, hoping to talk to him in private), Alan spends much of the play being the odd man out in this gay soiree. With his game, Michael hopes to out him, to force him to finally admit and own up to the damage he'd caused back in college to his friend Justin: "You ended the friendship, Alan, because you couldn't face the truth about yourself. You could go along, sleeping with Justin, as long as he lied to himself and you lied to yourself and you both dated girls and labeled yourselves men and called yourselves just fond friends." The motives for Michael's cruel game may be all too self-serving but they point to the emancipatory possibility such radical honesty could have in such intimate spaces—even if this Manhattan apartment is all the more hostile because of it.

As in *Perfetti sconosciuti*, the plot of *The Boys in the Band* is driven by a series of newly open secrets that reveal just how wounded their characters are. The drama at the heart of Crowley's play is its ability to confront the pain behind the very homophobia a character like Michael cannot escape. His apartment and the birthday party he throws stand in for the safe haven he and his friends have created for themselves. It makes sense Alan, a stranger, really, would disrupt their evening (and their intimacies, in turn). Crowley's play, which has been criticized for decades now for merely sketching out a portrait of bitter queens and self-hating fags, nevertheless presents a well-knit fabric of friendly intimacies that gay men in the late sixties could only find in private and within one another. What critic Ramzi Fawaz called "acidic" intimacies ("in the sense that they register the bitterness or sting of bonds cemented through shared knowledge of another gay man's insecurities, manipulations, and character flaws") structure the play's funniest lines. But also its most heartbreaking ones. Michael's oft-quoted witticism—"You show me a happy homosexual, and I'll show you a gay corpse," which he offers up as a quotation from someone, though he can't recall whom—feels both like a diagnosis of a larger ailment and a balm in itself. What drives Michael's game is the drive to out Alan, to himself and to the coterie of gay men assembled at the party. He fails, obviously. When Alan does pick up the phone to call someone he loves, he rings up his wife. It's unclear, to Michael (and us, really), whether Alan has retreated back to the safety of his marriage out of fear or out of love. In either case, what he accomplishes is a complete erasure of the evening as he's experienced it: when he leaves, he'll choose to forget he ever set foot in Michael's apartment. Michael can't forget, though. He'll be forced to face a world he doesn't understand, one he finds increasingly alienating. But one he can't run away from; he'll have to forge ahead.

If, as Adrienne Rich writes, an "honorable human relationship—that is, one in which two people have the right to use the word 'love'—is a process, delicate, violent, often terrifying to both persons involved, a process of refining the truth they can tell each other," then *Perfetti sconosciuti*, like *The Boys in the Band* before it, reminds us of the difficult paths we've forged for ourselves when we avoid being entirely truthful with those we love and who love us in return. But also about the understandable fears that fuel such decisions—and the fretful endings we careen toward when we let ourselves be truly known. The characters in *Perfetti sconosciuti*, unlike Albee's playfully cruel hosts, or Crowley's wounded, self-hating boys, are not allowed to imagine a life that would follow once all their secrets were aired out. Albee leaves us with an image of a broken couple at a crossroads, Crowley with a portrait of a man adrift who's unable to digest what he's unleashed. In both cases, these characters, and the audiences who have witnessed their derailed evenings, are encouraged to look within, to examine how they'd fare in such stressful evenings. You're left to wonder if you would have survived being hosted by Albee's George and Martha.

If you'd have picked up the phone and played Michael's charade. And, if so, what might you (we!) have learned from such bruising self-discoveries?

Honesty, it turns out, is the bomb that brings both plays to a standstill. Its damaging effects cannot be avoided; the aftermath may take place once the curtain falls but there's no running away from grappling with what we just witnessed. Genovese, in a seemingly cheeky move that feels all the bleaker, invokes a most tired of tropes: once the characters leave Rocco and Eva's house, we are led to understand that the game never took place. Each of the couples are yet again playacting their well-worn attentions, smiling about what a fun evening was had by all. Everything we have witnessed has been a "what if?" scenario, allowed, perhaps, by the magic of the full moon eclipse. No secrets have been uncovered. No affairs have been revealed. No coming out has taken place. Is that a happy ending or a dour one? Is the melancholy we're left with supposed to be comforting or disquieting?

Perfetti sconosciuti twists its title to remind us how little we know those around us and how little we can let ourselves be known, twinned anxieties that are rooted in the seeming self-evident truth that there are parts we wish to or can't help but keep to ourselves. But there's a way through this. And it may be painful, yes. Queer audiences surely understand that more viscerally than anyone else. We have had to live in a world where our greatest fear was to be openly honest about our life, about our desires—wants and needs that have been dubbed by many friends and family members (and many more strangers, in turn) as shameful and thus best kept to ourselves. In lumping Peppe's sexuality with Cosimo's many indiscretions, Lele's and Carlotta's dueling sexting exchanges, and even (yes!) Eva's own adultery, *Perfetti sconosciuti* broadens the concept of the closet to envelop all these other nonnormative intimacies.

In airing them out and having each of these couples confront what they're missing out on by not being honest with each other (and thus with themselves about who and what they want, who and what they want to be), Genovese's film opens the door toward a brighter, better world. The entire film stages a truly utopian possibility wherein no one is allowed to hide behind the thin veneer of respectability. Or propriety. Or shame, even. Honesty would seem to unshackle each of these well-adjusted adults from the many needless constraints that presumably push them toward ill-advised behaviors. But then it yanks all of that away. It cannot fathom a future for its characters following these disclosures and these revelations. It's an instructive ending that belies a lack of imagination.

For what would it really mean to live in that world? A world without privacy? Without secrets? Within an intimacy that extends beyond your couple and that's rooted in full-blown honesty, no matter how brutal it may be? "One of the central things we are looking for, as we look for love," philosopher John Armstrong writes in *Conditions of Love: The Philosophy of Intimacy,* is that we hope our "secret self should find a home in the eyes of another person, who will look upon this intimate aspect with pleasure." To love is to let someone else in and to let oneself be looked at nakedly, with abandon. That's not only thrilling but terrifying. And, as all these stories continuously remind us, remarkably unsustainable. For it suggests a stability of that secret self, of a private world, we can control and delineate with careful measure day in and day out. It's why strangers, perhaps, can look right through us with such candor and such relish. And why we may be tempted to estrange ourselves from who we are to our loved ones in hope there may yet be more secret selves to discover, more pleasures to be plumbed. Intimately. In private. And yes, sometimes in secret too.

4.
ON CRUISING

I AM CURRENTLY SITTING IN THE FOYER OF A HOTEL NEAR THE San Francisco airport. I'm hard at work on this book. I'm also, as the guy across from me notices just now, hard in that other sense of the word. I had hoped he'd notice. We'd been eyeing each other for a while. He'd gotten a drink at the nearby Starbucks and his imposing thighs, framed by delightfully short shorts, had first caught my attention, as had the white Nike Jordan Essentials tube socks that similarly hugged his well-sculpted calves. Novice that I am at cruising, I had worried the glances I kept catching from him were accidental. It's why I'd moved my laptop off my lap and given him a better view of, well, my actual lap. And so, next time he looks toward me in a casual way that doesn't let the girl friends he's with notice his distraction, I find his gaze landing on my right hand, which rests (quite seductively, I assure myself) on my clearly aroused dick. I rub it a bit. He licks his lips. And then, as if following a tacit script we both know by heart, he gets up, excuses himself, and heads toward the restrooms down the hall.

I don't—can't, really—hesitate. And so, despite the fact that I've been struggling to crank out my desired daily word count this week (I've been traveling a lot promoting my last book), I pack up my laptop in a rush to catch up with him. Only, by the time I enter the hotel's public restroom, he's nowhere to be found. *Damn*, I think. I must have miscalculated his interest. Which is a pity because if his legs (and freshly shaved angular facial features) were any indication, he'd make for a delicious notch in my budding hookup history. And so I take my place in front of one of the urinals and make as good use of this writing break as I can. It's then I see the door to one of the two stalls open; his smirk informs me he's very pleased to see me, if slightly annoyed that someone else in the other stall will limit what we can get away with. Standing side by side in adjoining urinals, we eye each other's cocks (he's clean shaven all over, it turns out). Eventually he's brave enough to reach his hand around and cop a feel—all before a slew of men walk in and break our makeshift intimacy. Outside the restroom he only spares himself enough time to tell me what is absolutely necessary. "Wait until I leave my friends. Then follow me upstairs: 4081."

Research, I tell myself, often comes from the unlikeliest of places.

When I first started telling folks that my next writing project would be all about the transient intimacies we can build with strangers, about the way in which brief encounters can be sites of endless possibilities, winks and nudges and snickers ensued. Oh how interesting that research would be, I was told. Talk about fun fieldwork, right? Friends enjoyed making me blush with such ribald ribbing. The truth was that at some point I would need to up my cruising game if I was to feel in any way prepared to engage intellectually with the ideas I was pursuing with this project. I'd need to put in hours in the field lest my entire chapter *on* cruising feel more like a sterile book report than an embodied (and, yes, well-researched) meditation on the joys of this queer practice. How else would I find whether cruising, as writers as disparate as Leo Bersani, Garth Greenwell, Tim Dean, and Marcus McCann have expounded these past few decades, was (is!) a different way of looking, a queer mode of reading, an example of impersonal intimacies, proof of a new vision of sociability? Or, more to the point of this project of mine, how could I confirm if cruising was, indeed, a welcome template with which to reframe how we connect with strangers?

Following the instructions of the young hot boy in the Jordan socks (white with a simple black "23" adornment, if you must know), I felt a novel thrill. I know, I know. "I've never done anything like this," sounds like a pickup line. A classic, truly. But in this case, it was true. (Not that I told him so; few words were exchanged, in fact.) One of my boyfriends—the one who can successfully cruise a boy while out washing the car or on a 7-Eleven run or sometimes even just on a walk—has long mocked me for my lack of experience in this matter. "It's so easy," he tells me often. "You just have to pay attention." He was right, as it turns out. Following the many pieces of advice he's given me over the last few months, I was able to connect with a guy in a public place with just eye contact and minimal body language and proceed to a second location with but a few words spoken in between. All I had to do was be open to what was around me. And to trust that I could make it happen. If I'd been less distracted by what was underneath the boy's black shirt and matching shorts, I might have asked him whether this was a regular occurrence in his line of work (he was a flight attendant). Whether, given the transience of his own everyday life, these kinds of furtive and fleeting encounters were all he ever comes to yearn or settle for. It's probably best I kept such indiscrete questions to myself. They would have revealed me as the bumbling novice I am. A novice in practice though definitely not in theory.

I first wrote about cruising in earnest for an undergraduate paper in an English class. Back in 2006, I was taking a course on gay literature and the syllabus included John Rechy's 1977 book, *The Sexual Outlaw*, which the author cheekily describes as "A Non-Fiction Account, with Commentaries, of Three Days and Nights in the Sexual Underground." From its opening lines, which talk of "streets, parks, alleys, tunnels, garages, movie arcades, bathhouses, beaches, movie backrows, tree-sheltered avenues, late-night orgy rooms, dark yards," and more, I was smitten. And intrigued. And mesmerized. And any number of other ways of describing what it feels like when a piece of writing cracks open the world for you. Rechy's sexual underground was revelatory for a twenty-one-year-old college boy who was slowly trying to make sense of himself as an out gay man in a whole new country, and who understood that as mostly consisting of falling for boys who openly flirted with him and dreaming up future lives with them, in turn. Amid such sophomoric ideals about what gay life could offer, Rechy's was a tempting proposition. After breaking up with my first-ever college boyfriend, I'd found a cute Aussie whose pop culture tastes neatly aligned with mine (a baffling dating requirement it's taken me much too long to let go of). And so, while I was reading about any and every filthy thing Rechy('s protagonist) did in the streets of Los Angeles in the 1970s, I was blissfully living out a rather square (homo)sexual experience. I'd told myself Rechy's "Jim" and his exploits on the page were an embalmed past I could never live out (hadn't such cruising died out in the eighties and nineties with the closure of bathhouses, with endless park raids, and a health crisis that discouraged if not outright vilified such practices?), and so I approached *The Sexual Outlaw* as a totemic text about an erotic fantasy as elusive and out of reach as any of the porn stories I used to read online in high school. Years later, this is but one of the reasons my then husband referred to it as my "porn book": it's a steamy affair, bound to elicit raised eyebrows and many a lingering look if you pull it out during your morning subway commute. When I first read it, I was bowled over. Never had a novel so turned me on while also intellectually stimulating me. I blushed at every other page, with shame, at times, but mostly out of a blissful kind of erotic and intellectual envy. Rechy didn't just effortlessly shuttle between the sexual and the political. He insisted we understand the two as dialectically intertwined. Not in an abstract sense where the personal *is* political but in an embodied way in which fucking could be a radical political act.

For cruising and hustling and scoring and "making it" in Rechy's world wasn't (solely) an excuse to drum up deliciously titillating scenes about fucking and fingering, about blow jobs and hand jobs, about orgies and one-on-one encounters. It was a cultural rallying cry. And, for a literary nerd with a penchant for queer theorization, the book proved to be a source of endless inspiration. Here was a way of apprehending so-called unsavory aspects of gay male culture in a productive way. Or so I told myself. In the comfort of a classroom and the safety of a college discussion where I could entertain deliciously debaucherous scenarios that I didn't dare live out in person. Out of fear, yes. And shame. And a distrust in my ability to conjure such possibilities. Rechy was the kind of gay man I aspired to be; his writing was the kind I aspired to live in. Failing in doing both, I settled for dissecting his scenes and ideas in my work. So much so that I ended up writing my undergraduate thesis on him and his book: "Rechy's documentary works to both represent and embody the cruising scene," I pompously expounded, following not just the Chicano writer's lead but the essence of one of my favorite Roland Barthes quotes: "I must seek out this reader (must 'cruise' him)," the French theorist writes, "without knowing where he is."

In my twenties, I could only think about cruising as an intellectual concept, one rife for interpretation and interpellation, one that
served less as a guide for sexual pleasures out on the streets and
more as a capable trope that helped me navigate what was happening on the sheets—on the pages, that is. In true undergrad fashion,
I quoted *The Joy of Gay Sex*: cruising is "going on the prowl and
looking for sex," the guide reads. Looking back, it's a paltry and
antiseptic description of cruising. Back then, and for much of the
two decades that followed, that's how I thought of cruising: with academic rigor but with an attendant distance. The closest I ever got
to dabbling in Rechy's "sexual underground" as an undergraduate
was shyly visiting the one bathroom in the main library on campus that I'd heard was a great spot to hook up, immediately feeling
much too sheepish about my presence there, and leaving before I
could corroborate the hushed whispers around it.

My brief fling with the flight attendant close to twenty years after reading about Rechy's scandalous exploits felt like vindication.
Sure, I'd been to bathhouses (back then always as a spectator; if I
saw and didn't touch, I could tell myself I wasn't breaking any of
my married life rules) and to back rooms and secluded gay beaches
and steamy dance floors (more recently, with my boyfriends in tow,
eager cheerleaders that they've become of my sexual escapades).
But *this* was novel. At last, and after years of thinking and writing
about Rechy's book (which later featured heavily in my doctoral
dissertation and even garnered a mention in my previous book,
The Male Gazed), I had a cruising anecdote of my own—a text-
book example of it, at that! All it required was a change in my own
orientation toward the world. My boyfriend had insisted that all I
had to do was pay attention. I had to be aware of my surroundings.
Everywhere could be a cruising space if you were attentive enough.
This is what Rechy teaches his readers. Not (solely) by showing us

how public parks and restrooms (and alleyways and piers and the like) make fertile ground for sexual encounters but by embodying the openness required to invite and entice such interactions. That's a lesson I'd learned from another book assigned to us in that gay lit class. William Beckwith, the protagonist of Alan Hollinghurst's *The Swimming-Pool Library*, doesn't so much reveal London to be a vast endless space for "cottaging" (the Britishism for cruising) as much as he reveals himself as the kind of person that makes such a description of London feel self-evident. William scores aplenty everywhere he goes because he's yet to meet a public space (or an attendant stranger) he couldn't lustfully turn on. Cruising, as Marcus McCann, author of *Park Cruising: What Happens When We Wander Off the Path*, puts it, is "a way of looking, a way of making yourself available to meeting people." But it is also "a way of being seen."

Cruising demands you reframe both how you gaze at the world and also how you invite the world's gaze. William is able to cruise boys everywhere in London because there are no spaces where cruising is not the desired goal. Witness him describing the tube: We're told he found it "often sexy and strange, like a gigantic game of chance, in which one got jammed up against many queer kinds of person. Or it was a sort of Edward Burra scene, all hats and buttocks and seaside postcard lewdery. Whatever, one always had to try and see the potential in it." Here lies the key to the cruiser: potential is everywhere if you so choose to seize it. Moreover, it requires understanding public spaces as rife for thoughts and actions that belong, we're often told, in private. It's why Hollinghurst cites Burra, whose early twentieth-century portraits captured a lascivious vision of urban life wherein sensuality was always on display (his *Soldiers at Rye* is no doubt the painting William has in mind given that it's composed of mostly round expectant buttocks and oversize hats, well, helmets). Hollinghurst moves us to think of the

London William observes as constantly being up for consumption, packaged for public viewing, postcards being the rare private correspondence that's open to be read by anyone who chances upon it. William refuses to observe any distinction between different public or private spaces: "Consoling and yet absurd," he muses later, "how the sexual imagination took such easy possession of the ungiving world." Sex, in William and Hollinghurst's worldview is—and could be had—everywhere. There is no fiction of such erotic intimacies as being corralled into the metaphorical "bedroom."

Hollinghurst's protagonist may well be a perfect embodiment, in all senses of the word, of the argument queer theorists Lauren Berlant and Michael Warner espouse in their infamous 1998 essay, "Sex in Public." Concerning themselves with how "heterosexual culture achieves much of its metacultural intelligibility through the ideologies and institutions of intimacy" (straight culture makes sex, for instance, something that only happens in the privacy of your own home between a socially sanctioned unit of two), their essay begins with a simple statement: "There is nothing more public than privacy." In their North American context—and responding quite vociferously to the arguments put forth by conservatives like Jesse Helms—Berlant and Warner saw how intimacies have been continually privatized. The passing connections Hollinghurst's William and Rechy's Jim so relish are socially disdained, if not outright criminalized. Narratives of love and family end up indexing the only available forms with which we're to be intimate with one another. Anything outside of that is marked, they argue, as other. As deviant. As criminal. But it's in those "criminal intimacies" that Berlant and Warner see rife potential: "girlfriends, gal pals, fuckbuddies, tricks," and the like are examples of close-knit relationships that are not easily legible within our socially sanctioned narratives (there are no "happily ever afters" in these stories, only, and even then just sporadically, "happy endings" at most). Queer culture, as they argue, "has learned not only how to sexualize these and other relations, but also to use them as a context for witnessing intense and personal affect while elaborating a public world of belonging and transformation. Making a queer world has required the development of kinds of intimacy that bear no necessary relation to domestic space, to kinship, to the couple form, to property, or to the nation." Against the invective that the only kind of intimacy one should value is the one you nurture at home, in the bedroom, with one other person, Berlant and Warner remind their readers that queer folks had been extolling the virtues of queer counterpublics and the tight-knit relations there created. In lesbian bars and gay tearooms, in cruising parks and public toilets, on piers and on the streets—even on phone sex lines and in softball leagues!—there's been no shortage of queer spaces where friendly, familial, erotic, and sexual relations have been championed. These are fleeting and fraught, mobile and transient as need be. But they are not, for that, any less important in helping to map out what, at times, feel like utopian visions of the kind of communities and relationships we could all be building.

William, who has but one close friend and barely puts any stock into his own familial relations, puts his energy in nurturing (however passing) intimacies with strangers. His London is rife with possibility precisely because he sees openings both literal and figurative wherever he goes. "There is always the question, which can only be answered by instinct," William tells us, "of what to do about strangers. Leading my life the way I did, it was strangers who by their very strangeness quickened my pulse and made me feel I was alive—that and the irrational sense of absolute security that came from the conspiracy of sex with men I had never seen before and might never see again." Those instincts, Will knows, are not infallible (a key scene in the novel occurs when, misjudging a possible score, he's beaten to a pulp by a group of homophobic neo-Nazis). But those instincts nevertheless structure his view of the world. Cruising is, at its most utopian, an equalizing practice that squarely depends on expecting the best (the most, really!) from strangers. This is what Hollinghurst stresses all throughout *The Swimming-Pool Library*: not for nothing does the inciting incident of the entire novel take place at a public restroom, where William unexpectedly finds himself saving an older man's life.

Hollinghurst's and Rechy's work—and here we should add the likes of André Gide and Jean Genet—feels particularly refreshing because depictions of cruising elsewhere in popular culture (and on the big screen, in particular) have tended to operate not under this generous reading of strangers but instead on their latent violent threats. And while that violence has a sensuous sensibility in the work of those two French authors—Gide and Genet arguably being the preeminent practitioners of a queer style where the erotic and the violent are literal and literary bedfellows—movies that have taken on the art of cruising have framed their narratives as crime thrillers rather than erotic ones. This includes not just William Friedkin's polarizing 1980 flick *Cruising* (itself loosely based on the same-titled 1970 novel by *New York Times* reporter Gerald Walker) but also Alain Guiraudie's equally steamy 2013 thriller *L'inconnu du lac*, known in English as *Stranger by the Lake*. In both films, the cruising world (respectively, New York City and a French lakeside beach) serves as backdrop for a murder investigation. The expansive social potentiality of cruising, of the intimate frisson that bars and beaches, streets and bushes offer, get reduced, instead, to possible crime scenes, dangerous sites that require policing. These films take that childhood safety mantra ("Stranger danger!") and infect it into spaces that otherwise depend on a sociability that's quite anathema to such strictures. Both protagonists, Al Pacino's detective Steve Burns, who goes undercover in the S&M and leather bar scene of the Meatpacking District, and Pierre Deladonchamps's Franck, who frequents a gay nudist cruising beach, are equally lured and unsettled by the threat of danger that soon enough permeates their daily routines. *Cruising* and *L'inconnu du lac* turn their lens toward sexual undergrounds not unlike those described by Rechy, though these films are suffused with requisite fear, each driving toward a disquieting denouement that reminds us no one is ever safe. But not before blush-worthy scenes that push the limits of what the big screen outside of hardcore pornography has comfortably depicted.

What's remarkable about looking at these two films side by side—and doing so while being keenly aware of the thirty years between them—is how the fear of promiscuous sex they each illustrate (if not outright engender) was, for the better part of the latter decades of the twentieth century, a lived reality for many gay men. The anxieties I myself struggled with about what it would mean to cruise someone in real life, be it at a campus bathroom or in a public park (let alone in bathhouses and sex clubs), stemmed from my teenage years—those years of budding sex(ual) education—being marked by an insistent fearmongering that collapsed gay sex with disease and with death. A year after *Cruising* opened, *The New York Times* first published its now infamous "Rare Cancer Seen in 41 Homosexuals" piece (July 3, 1981), while not even a year after *L'inconnu du lac* first screened in the United States at the New York Film Festival—which is where I first caught it myself—*New York Magazine* put Truvada on its cover (July 13, 2014), accompanying the aptly titled piece "Sex Without Fear," which discussed the way this new HIV-prevention drug would be revolutionizing sex for an entire generation. The three decades between *Cruising*'s leather bar–themed serial killer thriller and *L'inconnu du lac*'s nude, sun-dappled murder mystery enclose a specific historic moment when gay male sexual desire was policed in decidedly public ways.

It's been hard, no doubt, for many from my generation, those of us who find ourselves, as Mattilda B. Sycamore's edited anthology on the topic outlines in its title, as existing *Between Certain Death and a Possible Future*. Ours is a generational story, as Sycamore writes, that's rooted in having "come of age in the midst of the epidemic with the belief that desire intrinsically led to death, internalizing this trauma as part of becoming queer." Unshackling ourselves from the lessons of a recent history that had stopped feeling like an urgent crisis and faced with what may well be an open horizon where we can reimagine our attitude toward promiscuous sex, there are those who are only now belatedly coming to terms with what it might mean to cruise and fuck strangers with careless (or even careful) abandon. Especially because it requires letting go of a fearful approach to others, in contexts both sexual and not, that our culture ingrains in us with constant ease.

Cruising has offered fertile ground for critics, thinkers, and scholars alike. As a practice long criminalized and often degraded from within and outside the community, cruising has, over the last few decades, emerged as a kind of utopian practice that requires us to dream up more generative modes of relating to the other, to the stranger. In *Park Cruising*, McCann notes that the "defining characteristic of cruising is its porousness. Cruisers show deliberate vulnerability toward strangers." There's no way to make yourself available to others if you're closed off, something I've long been accused of being, or seeming (likely both). It's why keying into such a mood is difficult for me. For McCann, such porousness opens up a different way of conceiving of our sociability: "I often think," he writes, echoing the sentiment at the heart of Berlant and Warner's work, "of the ways which non-monogamous and queer people build intimate relationships not just with one or two people but as a kind of fabric whose interwoven strands overlap." The weaving metaphor is particularly helpful because it pushes back against the other image that's often deployed when we think of our public interconnectedness with strangers: networking. McCann's image is much more organic; it's a more productive figure too, with its own serviceable usefulness. But there's also an expansiveness to it: you could make plenty of different things with any one fabric. Those queered intimate relationships can and could be endlessly refashioned, repurposed—recycled, even. McCann notes that we should see a phrase such as "the strangers in your life" not as an oxymoron but as a kind of koan. It's an invitation to reassess why we so often feel compelled to revel in our estrangement from those we don't (or will ourselves not to) know. There's a tacit call toward empathy here, toward compassion. Filtered through lust, no doubt. But that makes the impulse no less ambitious. In his seminal treatise on cruising, *Times Square Red, Times Square Blue*, Samuel R. Delany helpfully teases out the tenets on which McCann's work is founded. Delany understands the distinct aspect of cruising, as "contact" rather than as "networking." This is why cruising is a concept inextricably linked with urban planning for Delany. Cruising is a practice that flourishes most acutely in densely populated areas where public spaces allow for such encounters to happen. The cruiser is an attentive observer of the urban world. And a rather active member of it as well. He moves through spaces with wide-eyed conviction that what he's looking for is out there, ready and willing to be enjoyed. What could we gain, then, by being open and opening ourselves up to strangers this way?

Such utopian considerations of cruising can leave one romanticizing the practice. Or a version of the practice. After all, nowadays, most queer folks encounter it mediated through screens where scrolling and filtering and blocking and ghosting have made it feel like an insidious way to know and covet others' bodies. What's lost in cruising for men on Grindr, say—or Sniffies, even—is the very contact with bodies Delany was so focused on. Such steamy tactility is lost when we're reduced to squares on a screen, to headless torsos with a laundry list of wants and needs distilled on first look. This is perhaps why I reach back to the work of Rechy and Genet and Hollinghurst and Gide to better arm myself with how best to bring a cruising attitude into my everyday (and obviously my sex) life. There I find a call toward soaking up bodies and stares, gropes and glances, in ways that push back against the antiseptic way of approaching men with a neutered "hey handsome" these apps so depend on and demand in turn. The very language of Rechy's work, for instance, demands you relish the many encounters he chronicles; he pulls you closer (cruises you, say) into a world where bodies do plenty of communicating.

The Chicano writer's breakthrough novel, 1963's *City of Night*, began as a letter to a friend. Never intended to be a short story (as many of its pieces first appeared in the *Evergreen Review*) nor as a novel (as it was eventually published by Grove Press), Rechy's writings began as a way to jot down the memories of his travels across America, "that vast City of Night stretching gaudily from Times Square to Hollywood Boulevard," as he puts it in the novel's first line. But they were directed to a friend, which explains, maybe, why Rechy's prose feels so intimate. He doesn't just immerse us in the hustling world he depicts but envelops us into its rhythms, making us willing voyeurs of the many erotic tableaus he constructs. In his infamous pan in the *The New York Review of Books* ("Fruit Salad"), Alfred Chester objected to Rechy's language: "The episodes are so gracelessly, clumsily written, so stickily, thickly literary," Chester protested, that "in his determination to boil every last drop of poetry out of pederasty, Rechy ends up with nothing but a pot of blackberry prose." In Chester's view, Rechy had "no ear whatsoever." Yet the critic's metaphor does capture something about the language in *City of Night*. It's sticky, for sure. Gritty and grimy, even. But also sweaty and sleazy. Take away Chester's decidedly homophobic put-down in equating Rechy's homosexual encounters with "pederasty" and you find precisely why he struggled to hear the poetry in this seminal (pun intended) book. Rechy's insistence on the sheer mundanity of his encounters, on a rather blunt (clumsy, even!) style throughout, was very much the point. There was no attempt to elevate cruising or hustling or scoring or "making it" here. Just a choice to depict that world in a way that revealed its own sinuous sensibility.

Garth Greenwell, our most staunch contemporary advocate for the literary merits and rhythms of cruising, has long argued that cruising and poetry are kindred practices: "Both poetry and cruising have a structure that is essentially epiphanic, offering the sudden, often ecstatic revelation of a meaning that emerges from the inchoate stuff of quotidian life." Indeed, *City of Night*'s sprawling narrative—which takes us from El Paso to New York and Los Angeles and San Diego and La Jolla and San Francisco and Chicago and finally to New Orleans, with many detours in between—is obsessively interested in that inchoate stuff. Every encounter—at a beach, in a motel, down a pier, in an alley—is an opportunity for Rechy to paint a detailed picture not just of the places where his "youngman" narrator moves through but of the people who make such encounters worth writing about.

What remains astonishing about Rechy's work all these decades later is the way it refuses the call toward narrative. All we learn of *City of Night*'s "youngman" is through his sexual exploits, through whom and how he fucks. The 1963 novel is a collection of sexual interactions, not so much episodic as epiphanic. It's through strangers that he finds self-knowledge and through sexual encounters that he builds out an identity for himself, one that's equally solid and slippery. The second-to-last chapter in the novel (and the last to be named after an encounter) is titled "JEREMY: White Sheets." Rechy's youngman is in New Orleans, enjoying Mardi Gras, like everyone else in the city. But there's a restlessness to the way our narrator is experiencing the carnivalesque world around him. The encroaching anxiety that has dotted his travels (and the many scores therein) is getting harder and harder to ignore. So much so that, before meeting Jeremy and going to a room to make it with him, he'd found himself dropping his "mask" and letting the two boys who were eager to take him home know that the indifferent image of masculine stoicism he was exuding was nothing more than a pose, one very much designed to attract boys like them and to guarantee his own desirability could never be questioned. "I want to tell you something before we leave," he had told them, "Im [sic] not at all the way you think I am. Im [sic] not like you want me to be, the way I tried to look and act for you: not unconcerned, nor easygoing—not tough: no, not at all." After many various attempts at tapping into his own vulnerability, Rechy's youngman (a fictionalized version of himself, remember) finally lets his mask crumble. That disclosure, though, had broken the spell: "Predictably, I became a stranger to them." In refusing to play the role expected of him, he estranged himself from their own fantasy and alienated them. It's why he ends up heading out with Jeremy instead—a way, he tells himself, to realign his sense of self. Such a score becomes a way to prove to himself that he could still don the mask that had elsewhere served him well.

Except, of course, what takes place in Jeremy's room, in between those white sheets, is ultimately a much more destabilizing reckoning. Their climatic dialogue forces Rechy's youngman to think back through the many scores and men he's left strewn all over the United States. And it allows the novelist to stage a dialogue that bristles with intuitive understanding between two people who know very little and yet so much about the other. "Do you always go for money—only?" Jeremy asks Rechy's youngman bluntly, a question that unsettles the novel's first-person narrator who is so rarely encouraged toward such probing self-awareness:

> "Yes," I lied. How impossibly difficult it seemed to explain to him that it was the mere proffering of the sexmoney that mattered, the unreciprocated sex: the manifestations that I was really Wanted [sic].
>
> "Oh?" he asked as if something in the way I had reacted so quickly has made him doubt it, perhaps, too—certainly—the fact that I hadnt [sic] asked him for money, that he had given it. "Somehow, listening to you with those two in the bar—and having seen you with others—I got the impression that the money they gave you wasnt [sic] the important thing—that you were, maybe, compulsively playing a game."

Such moments of discomfiting self-reflection stand in stark contrast with what's come before. *City of Night* depends on the accretion of its episodes and "JEREMY: White Sheets" is the novel's apotheosis, a moment both unique and mundane. In sum, it's a brilliant example of the radical potential of a cruising encounter.

Greenwell's work, including his novel *What Belongs to You* and a collection of short stories, *Cleanness*, dramatizes the electrifying possibilities of such cruising episodes. His work is an attempt to push back against the tired tropes that have long accompanied the discourse surrounding such practices. He combines two concepts (public and casual) that we're taught are antithetical to the kind of sex we are to privilege, value, seek out, and exalt, cruising has long been decried as a dirty, dangerous practice. In so doing, he's forced readers and critics to examine why such practices are seen as lacking depth, lacking value. In an essay titled "How I Fell in Love with the Beautiful Art of Cruising," Greenwell stresses, "There's no room in these narratives for what I've sometimes found in those spaces, which is an intimacy whose value is independent of duration, a lyric value, I'm tempted to say, which seems to me inexhaustible: moments of mutual recognition that are profound and merit reverence." This is precisely what transpires between Jeremy and Rechy's youngman. Priding himself on always being a cipher of a man whose own stoic reticence allows him to become a vessel for whatever is desired of and about him, the novel's narrator finds himself at a loss for words when Jeremy sees right through him. Or sees him, more like, precisely as who and what he is.

Here is intimacy remodeled and refashioned, a threadbare closeness that's discomforting because it's so acutely revealing. In revisiting Rechy's work in the context of this project, I most related to moments (however short lived) that stress what we looked for and found in the arms of strangers. Which is, ultimately, what *City of Night* is preoccupied with throughout. Rechy writes of the "cold intimacy" between strangers that follows movie house encounters; of the "crushed intimacy" you can witness while cruising in parks; of the "hurried intimacy" that only washes over you days or weeks after a score; and, of course, of the "anonymous intimacy" that so structures the world of cruising and hustling. He often follows such descriptions with the very word and concept that concerns me. After he wakes and finds Jeremy still lying in bed, the youngman frames Jeremy's offer of a cigarette in the way he often understands such gestures, "as if, I think, it were an indication of truce after the sex act which has suddenly, for me—now remembered vividly after the brief, blacked-out period of sleep—made us Strangers." Rechy's habit of randomly capitalizing nouns through his prose—the kind of literary tic that perhaps so irked Chester—should cue us here to really take up how writer and narrator deploy this specific concept. For it is everywhere in his prose, as if Rechy understood how central the semiotic porousness of the word *stranger* is for his project. If we follow Rechy at his word, the sexual intimacy that had just bonded Jeremy and *City of Night*'s youngman had, if ever so briefly, made them known to each other: they only became (were *made*) strangers once the blissful jouissance of such a moment evanesced.

When we first read *The Sexual Outlaw* in class, we had long discussions about what Rechy and his fictionalized surrogate were seeking in their seemingly endless sexual conquests. What drove a hulking, muscled tan man in tight denim to scour the streets for one hookup after the other? Why did Rechy so chase after, on the streets and on the page, momentary connections that left him adrift, wondering out loud to his reader whether any other kinds of bonds could be made between strangers in the night?

At every turn in *The Sexual Outlaw*, which notches hundreds of sexual encounters, Rechy seems to be running away from the possibility of encountering another Jeremy. "Jim" whisks himself away whenever he senses a closeness he wishes to expunge instead. For a character (and author) who so willingly gave his body away, those retreating gestures always struck me as indicative of something else; I even made the mistake of bringing it up once in class. "Don't you think that Jim is just afraid of intimacy?" The thundering laughter that greeted my all-too-earnest inquiry haunts me to this day. So much so that the specifics of how our professor rerouted the conversation away from my question have melted away in the decades since. What was clear was that shame-filled mockery was the only way to neuter my insistence on Jim's allergy toward intimate connections with his tricks.

Maybe what I was getting at was lost in translation, lost in the very language I am forced to use to make such questions legible. For Rechy's various autobiographical avatars *do* seek out intimacy. Though not the kind we tend to value when we use such a word in everyday life. Jim shows no reticence to finding closeness in and with strangers. But it's one devoid of the emotional vibrancy we call up when we think of intimacy within, say, a couple—married or otherwise. Perhaps my question, and the laughter it elicited in class, was indicative of the way this language fails us in understanding the myriad ways in which we can relate to strangers without falling back on known modes of relating to them. In *Unlimited Intimacy*, Tim Dean's groundbreaking study on barebacking subcultures in the late nineties, he asks a better version of the question I was getting at in trying to figure out why Rechy's Jim found closeness in distance throughout *The Sexual Outlaw*. It's a question that, like McCann's koan about the "strangers in your life," pushes us to (re)imagine a different relationship with and to strangers. It invites us to relish the porousness with which we can approach and understand them. And more importantly, it asks us to rethink how and what we construe strangers to be. It's a query that serves me, now, as the guiding principle of my cruising project, one that must be answered one score—one flight attendant with gorgeous calves—at a time:

"*Why should strangers not be lovers and yet remain strangers?*"

5.

NAKED FRIENDS

ATOP THE BOOKCASE IN MY LIVING ROOM SITS A FRAMED watercolor nude portrait. Every time I stare at it, I am transported back to the sunny Saturday morning it will forever capture. I can still feel the sweat droplets dripping down my back as I stood flanked by a wall of windows in a downtown New York City office space as if it had been yesterday. And not, as it turns out, close to a decade ago. I'd commissioned the piece for my then boyfriend who in time had become my legally wed partner and is now simply my ex-husband. Yes, I got to keep the gift in the divorce. Proof, perhaps, that there had been more than a narcissistic streak in this otherwise playful anniversary gift.

"What do you think your boyfriend will think of this?" the artist had asked me in an attempt, I realized, to ease me out of anxious stillness. Back then, I'd told myself that I had wanted to see myself anew. Rather, I wanted him, a stranger at that point (and a handsome one, at that) to help see me in a new light. I wanted to see myself the way he saw and drew his models. With a few ballpoint pen lines and some watercolor brushstrokes, he was able to conjure up an electric kind of dynamism. His pieces had stood out to me because of their alluring mix of raw sensuality and tender vulnerability. But I was also, I admit, intrigued by the scenarios they suggested.

One in particular was already on my mind. Decades earlier, like many other lovestruck teenagers who were bowled over by a certain sweeping romantic epic set aboard the most famous ocean liner, I had first learned about the intoxicating allure of figure portraiture. In *Titanic*, Jack and Rose (played by icy-blue-eyed teen heartthrob Leonardo DiCaprio and English rose incarnate Kate Winslet) didn't just offer a ready-made template for the alluring pull of a stranger who'd allow you to dream up a world and a life unlike the one you were being encouraged to pursue. They presented me with arguably one of the most indelible representations of the vexing relationship between artist and muse Hollywood has ever offered.

Hormones may have dictated I swoon for Leo, but when I left the theater with my sister after watching the three-hour epic for the first time, I was enamored with Winslet. Or rather, enamored with her Rose and the vision of desire she portrays on-screen. More than yearning to find myself someone who'd never let go, I left *Titanic* wanting to find someone who'd look at (and draw) me the way Jack does her. Someone who, even if I'd just met them (or because I'd *only* just met them) could allow me to refashion myself into the person I'd always hoped to become: to arrive a Rose DeWitt Bukater and emerge a Rose Dawson.

The first time we see Rose, she is but a sketch. Brock Lovett (played by Bill Paxton), a *Titanic* obsessive who's searching for the Heart of the Ocean diamond, examines a flimsy piece of paper. It's one among many that his diving crew retrieved from a safe that sank with the ship on that fateful 1912 maiden voyage. The paper is a portrait of a young woman. She's wearing nothing but the diamond that continues to elude Lovett. It is that same sketch that catches the eye of an older woman miles away who stops midway through her pottery and turns her attention to the TV, where a vision of herself stares right back at her. "Should this have remained unseen at the bottom of the ocean for eternity?" Lovett asks on a news broadcast, posing one of the many blunt meta questions director James Cameron litters throughout his screenplay. Little does he know that this older Rose (played by Gloria Stuart) holds the key to what he's long been seeking.

This portrait is the film: how it was created, how it ended in the safe, what it represents, what it obscures. Every question it raises is key to Cameron's plot of star-crossed lovers, as well as to the film's archeological interests. *Titanic* is a film about what remains, yes. About how intimacies, no matter how ephemeral, leave traces, how art can immortalize brief and chance encounters. It speaks to his interest in the history objects can tell. It helps, of course, that it is also at the heart of the film's most arresting scene—the one that left me agog when I first saw it and to which I return every time I revisit the film.

"I want you to draw me like one of your French girls," Rose tells Jack, the young man who first saved her from an ill-conceived suicide attempt and who has now seduced her enough to imagine a different future for herself, one far away from the well-to-do marriage arranged for her. Rose had complimented Jack on his sketches, many of them of Parisian women who had posed nude for him. "You have a gift, Jack," she'd told him. "You see people." For a young woman bemoaning the inertia of her life, one where no one really sees or notices her, Jack's perspicuity was not only endearing. It was exhilarating. By the time she disrobes and lies down on a couch in the pose we've grown so familiar with (in a sketch drawn by Cameron himself, no less), you can see why the image of Jack working away with his pencil was so ingrained in her memory. Before we ever see how Jack earned himself a ticket on the *Titanic*, we see his piercing glance from above his sketchbook haunting old Rose's memories as she prepares to tell her story. "Eyes on me," Jack instructs Rose. As Cameron's camera cuts between Jack's laser-focused attention and Rose's beguiled look, it strikes me that the reason the scene feels so erotic has nothing to do with Winslet's nudity. It has everything to do with the electrifying way in which Jack gazes at Rose. Not with lust, exactly (though he does blush). But not *without* lust. It's a fine balance. It's one I experienced that sunny Saturday morning when I lost myself in prurient thoughts, in the fabricated intimacy between a gay artist and a male model—at once too erotic to be utterly chaste, too demure to be outright sexual. Finally I could answer the simple question: What would it be like to feel that kind of gaze upon me?

As it turns out, it felt intoxicating.

The shirt had come off easily. As had the pants. And the socks, I guess. I had just pretended I was in a locker room, about to hit the showers at the gym. But once I got down to the briefs, there had been a moment of hesitation. A fluttering of anticipation. Once those were gone, there'd be nothing left to hide. That moment when I tugged at my briefs and took them off, a moment I'd always associated with either complete privacy or total intimacy, suddenly felt all too new. There was, it must be acknowledged, a performed awkwardness to what followed. But he had done all of this before; the piece I'd commissioned was nothing out of the ordinary for him. He'd seen plenty of dicks and bare asses. And while I was embarrassingly self-conscious (it's what happens when certain physical reactions cannot be, ahem, controlled), he made every effort to put me at ease. He's sweet natured and professional, I soon learned, at making this strange encounter with a stranger feel comfortingly familiar. Especially given how demure it remained, how little it spilled into more salacious territory.

We have no vocabulary to talk about the kind of intense intimacy that can be captured in nude portraiture without resorting to sexual innuendo. Whenever friends learn I've posed nude for artists and photographers, they raise their eyebrows and all but wink at me. Just as with *Titanic*, the assumption is that the connection between model and artist will have irrevocably led to more. But that's as much a failure of our collective imagination as it is a failure of how we codify intimacies that skirt the line of propriety within a society that conflates nudity and sex. This despite ample experience and examples (nude beaches and clothes-optional parties; Korean spas and nudist resorts) that stress such distinctions. Yet those spaces don't have the same pull for me as environments that demand not the ability to forget you're naked but the ability to acknowledge and pay close attention to said nakedness. It's the locker room without competition. The bathhouse without ulterior motives. The bedroom without insecurities.

After working on a number of warm-up ballpoint sketches, he eventually got to work on one of two watercolors he painted of me that day. I remember how my arms, both of which had been behind my head for more than twenty minutes for one pose alone, ached so much I almost considered asking him to pause. I didn't, though. I didn't want to break the spell of the meditative space we'd created between and around us. The eerie stillness made what we were doing feel all the more illicit than it should. Not illicit, I guess: titillating. As I surveyed the room, ignoring the pool of sweat gathering in the nape of my neck and all the way down my back, I focused on the space around me and tried to clear my mind. It was then that I landed on a line from one of my favorite poets, Frank O'Hara: "I am what people make of me—if they can and when they will."

It's that "if/when" clause that gets me. That calls to me.

The idea that we are what others make of us is not particularly novel. Such a sense of self is equally liberatory and constricting. To let yourself be defined by what others make of you (note the agency, the craftsmanship, here required) is to admit that there are times (always, perhaps) when we have no control over how we come across. We are social beings and thus our sense of self is constantly being interpellated by others; there's no way to know oneself without the help of other people. To understand that you're not just shaped by others but that no "you" can exist without them should put us at ease. That is, unless those others aren't really making of you what you hope to make of yourself. Which is where that if/when clause arrives.

By the time I showed up that Saturday morning to be sketched, I'd been thinking a lot about how I maybe wasn't all too comfortable with what people were making of me, with *how* they were making me. I was months away from leaving academia for good and I was starting to feel adrift; being a student (and a researcher, a teacher, a thinker, a scholar) had been central to how I thought of myself. What would be there when that part of me was gone? In tandem, I'd all of a sudden become a partner, a live-in boyfriend whose social life kept shrinking and whose social skills were atrophying. The social butterfly I'd become while in Vancouver had sniveled himself away, his queerness dimmed by his professional careerism on the one hand and his limited social circle on the other. I was living in one of the gayest cities in the world and yet I was feeling not so much closeted as embalmed in a vision of domestic bliss I kept trying to tell myself I wholeheartedly enjoyed. My world felt placid—stagnant, really. What better way to find (or forge or excavate or illuminate; you pick whatever ontological metaphor works best) than to find new people—strangers, more like—who could and would see me in a different light? And thus, who would make of me something I'd not yet become.

Frank O'Hara's greatest gift was the way he captured the immediacy of life. The lustful gaze that runs through his poetry all but demands you shed any shame you may have—about loving Lana Turner or wanting to fuck that cute guy you just met at the movies. His poems may seem like candid Polaroids, flashes of the present captured with casual ease, but they're closer to the detailed watercolors this artist I found myself bashfully posing in front of can create in a swift twenty minutes. If O'Hara's words came to mind it is because there's no way of uncoupling his poetry from visual art. Not only was the Baltimore-born poet a curator at the Museum of Modern Art (MoMA) in New York City in the 1950s, but many of his friends were celebrated artists in their own right. Who else can boast knowing John Ashbery intimately and having close friendships with the likes of Larry Rivers, Willem de Kooning, and Grace Hartigan, among others? Indeed, as I lived out my urbane fantasy of being drawn by an attractive man, I thought back to O'Hara posing for Rivers—a scenario that lives on in O'Hara's 1954 poem "On Rachmaninoff's Birthday" and, of course, in Rivers's famed portrait of the poet himself. In the poem, we get a sense of the playful rapport artist and poet had, of the electric intimacy they'd built over the years. He writes that he's glad Rivers made a statue of him, especially since his sculpted penis soon became all the rage among all those other young sculptors who'd seen it up close. O'Hara is boasting, of course. But he's also celebrating his friend's keen, attentive eye. As with many of the poems he wrote to and about his friends, here we find a brief missive about the joys of being seen by another. But beyond the carefully attuned friendship the poem illustrates, O'Hara's words offer us insights into a sexy confidence I hadn't realized I so coveted. One that was rooted in an altogether freeing way of relating to friends. Friends who could be lovers and witnesses and muses and interlocutors and vessels through which to explore every- and anything you would ever want to be. To become. But who'd remain friends nonetheless, if never more.

Upon his death at the young age of forty (due to an accident in Fire Island), his place of employment saw fit to celebrate him by staging an exhibit titled *Frank O'Hara/In Memory of My Feelings*. "It was decided that the best way the Museum might honor Frank O'Hara," René d'Harnoncourt, then director of MoMA, stated at the time, "would be the publication of a book of his poems decorated by the plastic artists with whom he was associated." The book and exhibit were, per d'Harnoncourt, "a homage to the sheer poetry—in all guises and roles—of the man." This kaleidoscopic vision of O'Hara included thirty poems illustrated by Jasper Johns, Elaine de Kooning, Roy Lichtenstein, Rivers, Hartigan, and many others. The book and exhibit understood how deeply O'Hara's work couldn't be disentangled from how he was viewed and (re)interpreted by his artist friends. As Russell Ferguson writes in that printed volume, "O'Hara's very sense of self was constantly refracted through his relationships with other people, their work and their needs." He was what others made of him (if they could and when they did).

This was very much the spirit expressed in the poem that gives the book and the exhibit its title. Dedicated to Grace Hartigan, the famed abstract expressionist painter, the poem opens with the concept of the poet's quietness having a man residing within it, which steers it, as a gondola. And no sooner has the poet offered up this bifurcated image of himself than he then further fractalizes it, telling us said man has several likenesses. "My quietness," he adds, "has a number of naked selves." Such plurality, so key to his work, is here laid bare. With every new line, these various selves stress how fractured O'Hara felt, reminding us how his poetry defied any calcified vision of the self. The equally simple and oblique impressionistic autobiographical poem—which itself became the basis for a Jasper Johns painting by the same name—brims with the concept of the self as constantly fragmented. Those various naked selves of his are scattered all over his poem but also in the many artworks he posed for. O'Hara may well be the most sketched poet of the twentieth century, having played muse to so many of his friends that the 1967 MoMA curatorial-cum-memorial exercise was but the first instance where entire exhibits could and would be centered around his portraits and collaborations in the 1950s and 1960s.

For a writer who so mined the plurality of his artistic self, the many portraits of him that exist stand not only as examples of his confident self-assuredness but the various ways his many friends saw him and how they each hoped to apprehend him. With Rivers, whom he wrote about plenty in his poems, it was clear that O'Hara felt like he would never need to hide; he let himself be openly seen by his friend. In 1957's "Two Dreams of Waking," he imagines a dreamlike scenario where he stands around naked for his artist friend: "'You think,' / Larry says, 'that you're safe / because you have a penis. So / do I, but we're both wrong.'" There's a sense of joint vulnerability. But also the sense that O'Hara highly admired his friend. It's telling that for the 1974 Vintage Books edition of *The Selected Poems of Frank O'Hara* (edited by Donald Allen), a Rivers nude portrait of O'Hara was used for its cover: the artist captured with his pen the raw vulnerability his friend brought to bear on his poetry. This is what makes *O'Hara Nude with Boots* (the painted version of that cover sketch) so entrancing. There's an androgynous effect Rivers draws out (and in) O'Hara. His friend is naked but he's kept his boots on. He's staring at us yet his pose (hands behind his back) feels coyly defiant. Much of the painting features bold brush-strokes that add to the hazy sense of the scene at hand, yet "O'hara [*sic*]" is neatly and plainly spelled out in the left bottom corner of the 97" by 53" portrait. And then, of course, there's the cinder block on which his right foot is leaning. There's a constructedness to this pose even as it conjures a casual interaction. You almost get the sense the two might have come up with the entire idea after having sex. For yes, it does bear pointing out, after all, that Rivers and O'Hara, who collaborated on several pieces (including the ten-part lithograph series *Stones*), were often lovers. In fact, they kissed the very first night they met, at a John Ashbery party in 1950: "He was a charming madman," Rivers writes of O'Hara in *What Did I Do?*: "a whoosh of air sometimes warm and pleasant, sometimes so gusty you closed your eyes and brushed back the hair it disarranged." Whether you read the poet's mentions of Larry ("How lucky we are that you're in so many museums so we can go and look and be out of traffic," he writes in *Stones*) or stare into the artist's paintings of his poet friend, what's unmistakable is how nakedly they saw each other. How unguarded they were able to present themselves *as* their various selves to each other. Theirs was a friendship that brimmed with an erotic porousness that's hard to categorize. And one that Rivers, apparently, at a time when he imagined his friend was getting much too attached, tried to end. A scathing letter set him straight soon after: "If you were busier about other things than trying to imagine my feelings you might stop complicating one of the simplest and least troublesome little affairs you've ever had," O'Hara fired back, settling whatever confusing sexual thoughts his artist pal was wrestling with in his head.

That sun-dappled morning when I posed for my own portrait

was but an attempt to construct a kind of friendship Rivers and O'Hara model for us in their work. My purpose then—to be so seen by someone who is not our lover (but isn't, doesn't have to be, not *not* your lover)—was a tad self-serving. Worried that I was too caught up in my own thoughts ("You're so still," I remember him telling me), the artist at work tried to steer the conversation into relatively safe territory. He regaled me with stories of how he'd painted several couples in the past to celebrate similar milestones. Except, of course, in this case, there was no couple. Just me. I had initially wondered if my boyfriend would've been up for such an adventure. After all, he had the more toned body (thanks to the kind of discipline about gym routines and pre-/post-workout shakes I envied and resented only slightly). Moreover, he seemed unencumbered by the self-consciousness I sometimes felt while naked even in the privacy of our shared one-bedroom apartment. I tried to not think too much about what he would've answered had I offered him such an invitation; perhaps because I selfishly wanted this intimate moment all to myself. In a way, I tacitly understood that what he made of me was what was in dire need of being redrawn. It was then, while in the middle of dipping his brush onto the canvas, the artist asked what my boyfriend would make of the gift, a question he immediately noticed caught me off guard. "I don't know," I mustered. The hesitancy he could hear in my response came from a place of, I must admit, shame. No, here what haunted me was shame's Spanish equivalent: *pudor*. It's apt not only because it's the language of my family and my homeland but because it's one letter away from *sudor* (sweat). *Pudor* is a visceral reaction. Something deep in me wanted to tarnish this moment, couldn't help think of it as being stained with prurient embarrassment—with what *púdor* represents: a modesty rooted in notions of what's appropriate and what's allowed. Of course, as a thirtysomething gay man who was living in a big city, the very thought of feeling shame at having displayed my body so unabashedly in a decidedly private environment struck me then (and even more so now) as timid at best and prudish at worst. Neither gave me any comfort.

The more I think about it, the more that morning's artistic session felt like a bumbling attempt at unpacking what I really wanted this gift to mean. To say. To stand for. On first look it seems, especially now that it graces my living room, rather self-serving. Yet at the same time, posing for a nude portrait necessarily requires vulnerability, giving up control. It's about letting go of your own sense of self and letting someone else reveal it to and for you. It's quite fascinating to reflect on the way we're encouraged to only ever so reveal ourselves to those we do (or want to) have sex with: nakedness remains constrained to the world of sexual intimacy.

What would it mean to uncouple nakedness from sexual intimacy? Or, conversely, to make more room in friendships for the erotic potential of naked encounters? Here's where O'Hara's own coterie of artist friends stands as a welcome template. Already by 1965, in an exhibit by Wynn Chamberlain, O'Hara's nude portrait stood alongside those of Ruth Kligman, Allen Ginsberg, Peter Orlovsky, Diane di Prima, and Bill Berkson, among others. In fact, in the 1964 double portrait titled *Poets Dressed and Undressed*, Chamberlain had illustrated Joe Brainard, Joe LeSueur, Frank Lima, and O'Hara twice in ostensibly the same pose: three of them sitting, one standing behind. In one portrait, all four poets are dressed quite smartly in matching white shirts, dark blue pants, and black ties. Their expressions, against the simple and flat-looking blue-and-green backdrop, are solemn. Together, they're a portrait of professional respectability. In the other, all four are naked and their serious frowns have been turned upside down into gleeful smiles. According to Ferguson, who reproduced both portraits in

In Memory of My Feelings, Chamberlain's diptych "overtly invokes the playful quality that some gay men of the period could bring to the masking and unmasking that was an unavoidable part of their lives." The freeing openness of the poets' nudity was, in Ferguson's view, inextricably linked to their experience as gay men in midcentury America. It's no accident Ferguson echoes in his words the very concept that opens O'Hara's 1954 poem "Homosexuality." Masking, here taken both literally and figuratively, plays a part in O'Hara's poetic imagination. To reveal oneself, whether in taking off one's clothes or letting oneself be truly seen (the one indelibly intertwined with the other) was an act of stripping, of letting go of the social accoutrements that make up our everyday lives.

I still remember the fluttering sense of recognition I felt when I was first shown the final watercolor, the one I'd later frame and hang on our—and then just on *my*—wall. It's odd to see oneself amid brushstrokes and lines. To see every muscle, hair, and mole pointedly looking back at you from what was once a mere blank page. There may be no boots and no cinder block, but there was no denying that, inadvertently, we'd created an echo of Rivers's 1954 portrait of his poet friend, the aptly titled *O'Hara Nude with Boots*. And, just as in the artist's depiction of O'Hara, who seems both defiant and at ease in equal measure, there's a welcome confidence I witness in this finished sketch, which in turn triggers another line from O'Hara's "Homosexuality," a poem I so adore. It's a line that I now consider to be the portrait's unspoken, if sly, caption—as well as an aspirational motto I've yet to comfortably inhabit and that I aspire to on the daily:

> It's a summer's day,
> and I want to be wanted more than anything else in
>   the world.

This is what Allen Ginsberg had articulated in the program for Chamberlain's nude portrait show. The gift Chamberlain had given the beat poet was the ability to see himself in a way he'd once been unable to, a reaction to seeing his own nakedness through someone else's eyes. Ginsberg confessed he'd always thought of and saw himself as ugly. No more: "I no longer look at myself through my own eyes, I look out—my eyes look outward at my Desire, and I reach out to touch the bodies I love without fear that I'll be rejected because I'm ugly. Because I don't feel ugly now, I feel me—more than that, I feel desirous, longing, lost; mad with impatience like fantastic old bearded Whitman to clasp my body to the bodies I adore." Many of us, no doubt, have found what Ginsberg felt in the gazes of others. But we expect them to come from the looks of those we love—or those who love us in return. The gift the poet finds in his nude portrait, and now in his own nudity, is the ability to have decoupled it from such romantic intimacies. He's found a new way to look at himself that's derived not from romance but from desire, a desire couched within the confines of friendship.

When I first daydreamed about posing just like Rose had, my mind could only fast-forward to the more salacious interactions between the brassy young gal and the penniless artist who'd seduced her. Or I thought back to those late nights during college when, armed with a cheap webcam connected to my laptop, I'd let myself be ogled by endless strangers whose commands I so enjoyed toying with on any given day (or night). But such moments of nudity, couched in anonymity and unruly desires, were miles away from what I experienced that morning with my hands up and sweat trickling down my back. I had, I realized, very little control over the situation; I was object, not subject. Such an admission was empowering and flattering at the same time.

Posing for a nude portrait necessarily requires a lack of vanity that seems to go against the very narcissistic impulse we associate with wanting others to ogle our naked bodies. By agreeing to become the subject of such a portrait, you leave your body and your vulnerability at the mercy of the artist. Perhaps the narcissistic impulse gets shifted, as it becomes flattering to think of oneself as a muse and as a future object to be lusted after. Much like the rapt audience who listens to old Rose's scandalous story about posing for Jack, people seek reassurance that the interaction between model and artist is entirely professional. Despite it never spilling over into more sexual territory, I still feel the hint of eroticism whenever I tug at my briefs and take them off in front of an artist. Yes, there's still the novel feeling of stripping, but there's also the knowledge that the moments I'll spend with them will encourage a feeling of being both wholly present and absent. In many ways, one grounds oneself in a pose. But as the artist is the one at work, posing encourages a wavering and wandering mind. It's a moment of intimate connection that is also dependent on boundaries and distance. In one's nakedness, one hopes to dispose of any posturing; in the stillness of modeling, one cannot help but do so. That's why Rose's gaze seems aimed at but also stretches far beyond Jack. It's why, upon seeing the finished sketch (which is a far cry from the impressionism of Monet and cubism of Picasso, both artists we know she adores), she cannot help but be moved. Per Cameron's screenplay, "He has X-rayed her soul."

That's no doubt what every figurative artist aims to do: to capture something ineffable with a few lines, with a few brushstrokes. But Cameron's words, with their nod to more technologically advanced equipment, nudge me to realize how much photography can help us look at ourselves anew. Given its presumed impersonal objectivity (a mirage, of course), you can't deny how a candid shot—or, say, a professional headshot taken by a flirty photographer—can illuminate something about you that you were maybe hiding from yourself. In addition to drawing and painting me that Saturday morning, my artist friend took a number of photographs of me. In the nude, of course. In one, with my arms crossed over my chest, my eyes alighting on something just slightly afar in the horizon, I am almost unrecognizable—especially once he used it as a reference for a red chalk drawing that remains the most flattering portrait he's ever sketched of me. Those sinuous muscles and those pronounced obliques feel like they belong to someone else; they capture as much how he saw me that morning as how I could potentially see myself. There's an enticing beckoning call in its simplicity—not unlike the kind Jack hastily illustrated when staring into Rose's eyes. Perhaps that's what makes Rose's portrait all the more alluring: her eyes are squarely locked with ours. They project a wounded vulnerability that's erotically charged (she is naked but for a necklace, after all).

Such a gesture, of a languid pose asking us to inch ever closer to its subject, is perhaps even more pointedly titillating not when it apprehends a young woman in the throes of desire (as in Rose's case) but when it frames a young man at home in his own bed, in his own skin. I think, for instance, of Peter Hujar's 1981 photo of his friend, *David Wojnarowicz Reclining (II)*. Shirtless, with tufts of his chest hair peeking behind his crossed arm (a perked-up nipple clearly visible from within the black-and-white shadows that texture the image), the image of Wojnarowicz hinges on his casually indolent expression. With a pillow right behind him, the close-up photo asks us to bask in the intimacy Hujar and Wojnarowicz have created together. It's the kind of portrait that's belatedly granted the late twentieth-century photographer of a queer and queered New York City the outsize reputation he deserved. "Like Peter's own face, the face of Hujar's art is both handsome and hurt" is how

Stephen Koch, who became the executor of Hujar's estate after his death of AIDS-related complications in 1987, puts it. There's a tension in his work that pulls you in and yet keeps you at a distance. "The tension one feels in these pictures is a magnificent aesthetic expression of what people invariably felt around the man. Nobody who spent more than an hour around Peter is likely to forget that Hujar edge, cutting into the very air around him, everywhere and always." That edge, in a piece like *David Wojnarowicz Reclining (II)*, comes through as necessarily in conversation with something softer, with a honeyed closeness with his subject (it's the parted lips, the centrality of a hairy pit, of his half-closed eyes), a fellow rage-fueled artist whose work he'd continue to inspire even after his death. In nakedness, Hujar could always be counted on to orchestrate a tense and terse encounter that nevertheless hinted at more, that beckoned you in.

A few years after I'd first posed in the nude, a friend hosted a World Naked Gardening Day party. Yes. Such a holiday does exist. And yes, to answer your question, it did involve gathering a group of willing queer folks eager to drop trou and enjoy an afternoon rejoicing in the joys of gardening—all while producing, collectively, what became my friend's print magazine turned online community-space, *Natural Pursuits*. If posing for one artist had first introduced me to the titillating feeling of being seen in a chastely erotic way, this nudist party clarified something that wasn't as obvious at first. As I stared around at the naked queer men around me, I realized how misguided my own conflation of desire and intimacy had been. After all, many of us are only ever naked with others when seeking sexual intimacy. Once that's out the window, it's easy to see how silly it is to ever equate the erotic with the sexual. Rose, in fact, had made the same mistake. When she first sees Jack's nude drawings, she tries to make sense of the intimacy Jack had captured in the only way she knows how. "I think you must have had a love affair with her," she suggests. "No, no, no, no," he protests. "Only with her hands."

When I first saw the scintillating scene between Rose and Jack in a darkened theater in Bogotá, I craved finding someone who'd look at me the way Jack stares at Rose. First, from afar, when he catches her eye on the deck, and later on, of course, as she lies naked before him. What I didn't quite understand was that those gazes need not be found only in sweeping romantic epics. Despite Cameron's cloying ending (where a young, presumably ghostly, Rose meets up with her 1912 paramour in a restored *Titanic* populated by all the people who died on its maiden voyage), the story of Rose Dawson didn't end with that icy-blue-eyed heartthrob. As the pictures next to her bed attest, she lived a full life, with many romances and adventures beyond the tragedy she witnessed in the Atlantic. The portrait and the love story is pivotal. But more for what it taught her than for what it was. Right before she gets a look at Jack's Parisian sketches, she bemoans the way her life ahead feels much too small; a marriage has been arranged, "and all the while," she says, "I feel I'm standing in the middle of a crowded room screaming at the top of my lungs and no one even looks up." It explains why the moment when someone paused to see her—to really see her as she wished she could be seen and desired—stayed with Rose for so many more decades. Jack gave her the gift of feeling seen, which is exactly how I feel whenever an artist's eyes trail their way down my own body. It's as addicting as it is nourishing, and I don't even have to suffer through an iceberg to feel the erotic weight of that gaze. A memory to tuck away when you're feeling down, or ugly, or unwanted: "It was the most erotic moment of my life," Rose confesses. "Up till then, at least." I viscerally understand what Rose felt. I return to her feeling time and time again; in fact, there's a voice in my head that rattles O'Hara's "I want to be wanted" line at me over and over again whenever I find myself relishing the eroticism of offering up my body to others—in photos, in poses, and, yes, sometimes even in real life.

That American poet always knew that clarity was found in simplicity. His conversational style makes reading one of his poems feel like you are chatting with an old friend—one as likely to talk about Cokes and lovers as about movies and cruising. It's that latter bit that takes up much of "Homosexuality." The joy of a summer's day for O'Hara necessarily required scouting the scorching streets of New York City for a throng of boys eager to see and be seen, to feel and be felt, to want and be wanted. Even in its abstraction, the poem captures the vexing feeling of such desires. Of that need to see yourself through someone else's eyes; someone who, without any words, will make you feel beautiful. And admired. But, above all else, someone who'll make you feel fuckable. I've slowly come to realize that such a someone can be a stranger (sure) but also, even, a close friend. That shouldn't be as surprising a statement as it reads. After all, why should we scrub eroticism from our friendships?

At O'Hara's funeral, Rivers shared how he always felt like he was the poet's best friend. "There are at least sixty people in New York who thought Frank O'Hara was their best friend," he further deadpanned. It's a line that speaks not just to the poet's jovial openness but of the varied and intimate connections he made throughout his life. The kind that live on now, not only through his poems (many of which he dedicated to and wrote about his friends) but in the portraits and sculptures and photos and books and cartoons he inspired. Years later, photographer Nan Goldin would say the same thing at the funeral of another famed queer New York City luminary: "The thing that was most amazing at Peter's funeral was how many people came who thought they were Peter's best friend," she wrote in 1994. Goldin was referring, of course, to Hujar, a fixture of the downtown art scene in the seventies and eighties who inspired and influenced her as well as an entire generation of artists with his striking black-and-white photography (particularly his portraiture; his most famous works include photos of Susan Sontag, Andy Warhol, Candy Darling, David Wojnarowicz, Paul Thek, and Fran Lebowitz). Speaking of his nudes in particular, Goldin added the following: "His pictures are exotic but not in a shallow, sensational way. Looking at his photographs of nude men, even of a naked baby boy, is the closest I ever came to experience what it is to inhabit male flesh." She was keying into the empathy his lens afforded his subjects and the way his gaze, at once tender and erotic, probing and impersonal, managed to capture a nakedness that went beyond the nudity on display.

Goldin's remembrance of her friend was collected in the 1994 book *Peter Hujar: A Retrospective*, which collected testimonies and memories from many of the photographer's coterie of artist friends alongside a curated selection of Hujar's work. Much like MoMA's O'Hara memorial-exhibit-cum-poetry-collection, that printed retrospective made clear that Hujar's work could not and would not be disentangled from the relationships—the friendships, really—that were all over his work. Every anecdote shared (like fellow photographer Gary Schneider recalling the days when he'd play protective voyeur at the piers as Hujar cruised and took pictures; or filmmaker/actor John Heys confessing he'd made love in front of and behind Hujar's camera) stressed the closeness Hujar's lens constructed. In writer Robert Levithan's words, "The pouring over the contact sheets might be cerebral and professional, but the act of picture taking was always intimate, tender—often erotic or overtly sexual." This is what made Hujar's portraits all the more striking:

they managed to capture a candidly posed vulnerability, one that atomized his subjects into their most elemental selves.

The first time I saw Hujar's photographs in person was at the Leslie-Lohman Museum of Art in 2014, but a few months after I posed for that watercolor portrait and later for a few photographers in the weeks that followed. As part of the museum's *Permanency* exhibit, the curators had presented a triptych that had *Seated Nude, Bruce de Sainte Croix* (1976) being flanked by *Standing Nude: Bruce de Sainte Croix* (1976) to its left and *Bruce de Sainte Croix Masturbating* (1976) to its right. I was then struck by the erotic stillness they captured. Yet seen together, they felt like an inadvertent (and rather irreverent) comic strip wherein this young Bruce fellow offered up his body for our consumption but without the attendant leering lasciviousness you'd dream up if you went only by their helpfully descriptive titles. Four years later, I'd encounter that central image again at the Morgan Library's *Peter Hujar: Speed of Life* exhibit. In the spring of 2018, that far-reaching retrospective featured plenty of photos I'd seen and admired before, like that reclining Sontag portrait and that *Christopher Street Pier (2)* image, which has, now for the last few years, served as my iPhone lock screen (I adore the subtle eroticism of its denim shorts, socks, and boots combo). But I was most struck—and how could one not be?—by *Seated Nude, Bruce de Sainte Croix*, there truly standing out on its own. Beautifully composed, the black-and-white photo features a young, naked man, seated on a wooden chair against a spare room. One hand rests on his abdomen, the other grips his fully erect penis. His gaze is downward cast, leading us to wonder what it is he's thinking as he calmly observes his tumescence. As with most of Hujar's portrait work, the classic composition and the interplay between light and shadows is arresting.

The photo is neither aggressively sexual nor chastely erotic.

There's a meditative quality to it, one that necessarily disrupts however one should feel about, well, a photo of a guy holding on to his perked-up dick. Helpfully, the Morgan Library offered a brief annotation for the photo: "Ste. Croix explained, 'I had been a dancer, and I was used to being an object in other people's art. [This time] the dance was to be a young man with an erection, and naked.'" Such simplicity is echoed in many a Hujar anecdote where his work calls up an ease of authenticity filtered through a performance. *Seated Nude, Bruce de Sainte Croix* had first been shown as part of the Marcuse Pfeifer Gallery's *The Male Nude in Photography* exhibit in 1978. Well, "shown" is a misnomer given that Pfeifer kept that Hujar pic sealed in a box for those who wished to see it (it was understood that it was truly that scandalous); but the print eventually became the best-selling one in the entire show when Hujar allowed it to be reproduced alongside what was, alas, a scathing review of the show in *The Village Voice*. To Ben Lifson, the entire exhibit was aimless. And not even Hujar's photos (which he'd often thought of as "overly theatrical") could rise above the risible attempt to normalize male nude portraiture: "The nude in art is a matter of convention," Lifson had argued. "In photography it's difficult because everyday experience doesn't readily proffer naked people to say nothing of men with phallic symbols between their legs; a nude in a photograph is presumed naked in order to be photographed." What followed was a rather tepid attempt at suggesting that male nudes didn't lend themselves to abstraction in the same way that female nudes had and did. Hujar's "awkward masturbators" make "the idea of solitude—always latent in a portrait—part of the explicit experience and meaning of his pictures." That *Seated Nude, Bruce de Sainte Croix* was front and center in Lifson's printed review made it hard to take his argument seriously. And not just because of its specious gender politics.

Studying the photo *The Village Voice* captioned as "all Priapus and no garden," I see not solitude but impersonal intimacy. Hujar is right off frame but, given the emptiness with which he surrounds Bruce (as he does in most of his works), there's a way in which he encourages us to zero in on his subjects and to see them with a newfound gaze. They're strangers you're called to get to know intimately. There's a call toward closeness that depends on distance. This was, in a way, what had first drawn me to those pen-sketched watercolor nude portraits that led me to pose nude. The finished portrait, which I've been stealing glances at all through writing this chapter, remains a reminder of how the gazes of strangers drive me wild. They pull me out of myself and out into a world where I can feel comfortable in my own body, with little shame to show for it. Those confident brushstrokes spell out my desire to be desired by whoever is staring at the painting, at my body, at myself.

6.

CLOSE FRIENDS

YEARS AGO, MY NOW EX-HUSBAND GAVE ME A CARD WHOSE playful cover soon became a mantra of sorts for our relationship. I even recycled it and made it an integral part of a series of photo collages that sat for years as magnets on our fridge. "A Best Friend You Can Have Sex With," the card read. I loved its cheeky message. Loved the way it helped make legible how we saw each other. The card was a promise. As well as the premise of how we understood our shared companionship.

One time, when my sister was visiting, she pointed at the collage and admitted that this was what she longed for in a boyfriend herself. I could see the appeal. When we think of long-term companionship, many of us have similar ideas in our minds, though it is rarely so simply spelled out. And at the risk of giving a greeting card more rhetorical importance than it likely deserves, I admit that having my relationship so neatly distilled was emboldening. Now, though, when I stare at that description, I can't help but tease out how it might unhelpfully frame a romantic dynamic. How it can blur it, in fact. And needlessly splinter it in half. You need friendship and you need sexual chemistry. If you add the two, you'll get something else. But maybe the sum could and would never be larger than its parts. For implicit in its formulation was a winking lack of imagination: Couldn't you very well have sex *with* your best friend? Moreover, why was the card framing this as a kind of permission? By and for whom? And, at a broader level: Why would friendship be necessarily siloed away from erotic attraction?

Such necessarily pedantic questions (about a card likely picked up from a stack of more inane-sounding ones at a CVS ahead of one of our many celebrated anniversaries) plague me for how neatly they illustrate deep-seated ideas about how friendship and romance (or friendship and lust, more like) are necessarily divorced from each other. My musings on friendships (queer friendships, in particular) have been spurred by my own journey—at nudist gatherings and back rooms at dance parties, on Twitter and in Instagram DMs, at book clubs and poker games, online and IRL—where I've seen firsthand how inadequate our equally narrow notions of such friendly bonds can be. My thirties, much of them spent in New York City, opened me up to a whole new way of conceptualizing what a friend could be, what a friendship could look like. Not in contradistinction to the romantic and sexual partnership I already had but as complementary to it. But this query began in earnest when I was faced with an appropriately named social media feature.

In late 2018, Instagram, that ubiquitous photo-sharing social network, released an update that would upend the way public and private intimacies were codified in online spaces. "Close Friends" was a feature that would allow users to self-select a number of their followers with whom they could share more private Stories (those vanishing posts that had supplemented Instagram's grid aesthetic). In essence, the arrival of Close Friends lent users the ability to carefully curate different online disclosures; some could be made for all to see, others could be more selectively shared. It affected what we offered up of ourselves and to whom.

In an August 2022 piece in *The Atlantic*, writer Jennifer Miller teased out why so many users had been expertly exploiting this most attractive of user features. Quoting various folks who explained how they leveraged Close Friends to have meaningful conversations about *Roe v. Wade*, share drunken exploits without worry about mean-spirited commenters, and even post missives on depression knowing they'd be heard by a sympathetic audience, Miller posited that the reason why users embraced this feature was trust. It allows you to curate an audience where you know your message will be welcome by those you've chosen as your Close (though, note, not clos*est*) Friends: "The feature's advantage is that it mitigates the effects of what social scientists call 'context collapse—the idea that on social, there's a flattening of multiple audiences in one space,' Elia Powers, an associate professor in the mass-communication department at Towson University" tells her. Creating a Close Friends list is akin to artfully planning a dinner party of like-minded guests. It's a way to make sure your inside jokes, your cultural references, and even the tone of your post will be rightfully understood—celebrated, even. All while everyone enjoys a lovely time together.

Curiously absent from Miller's brief overview of Close Friends is the way in which I (and many a queer man I know) use this function to further restrict who can view certain kinds of content we post. Namely: nudes. Not full-frontal ones. Those remain, per the app's most recent community guidelines ("Post photos and videos that are appropriate for a diverse audience"), squarely prohibited: "We know that there are times when people might want to share nude images that are artistic or creative in nature," they read as of August 2024, "but for a variety of reasons, we don't allow nudity on Instagram. This includes photos, videos, and some digitally created content that show sexual intercourse, genitals, and close-ups of fully nude buttocks." Said "variety of reasons" have been, for years now, notoriously opaque. But given that by definition Close Friends posts are targeted at the opposite of the "diverse audience" that your public photos and stories are, they've become a welcome safe space for some decidedly not-safe-for-work (though ostensibly tasteful) content. To this day I still bristle when I find a green circle post featuring things as inane as meals or kids—politics, especially. Friends and followers have trained me, instead, to expect post-workout mirror photos at the gym in compression shorts, athletic gear, or maybe even less; shower shots where steam or towels leave something to the imagination; pool pics where curves and ridges are easily discerned; and any and all variations on said themes (in beds, balconies, hotel rooms, you name them).

There is no mistaking what kind of context those of us who use Close Friends this way are creating. There's a playful (friendly, even!) vibe to it, where we egg one another on to flatter and flirt. Every Close Friends photo I post is an invitation. A come-on. A wink. I still do not have great IRL cruising game (though I'm working on it). But give me ten or so minutes in front of a mirror armed with my iPhone and a tight pair of briefs and I can mobilize enough men's "fire" emoji reactions to eventually snare the kind of flirtatious sexting conversation that can help me pass the time and reassure me that I am, in fact, wanted. Not only by strangers but also by not *not* strangers. The Close Friends list I've amassed is an odd mix of what we might call actual friends (folks I see regularly and socialize with, keep in contact with, and make a point of connecting with offline on occasion), and acquaintances (local and virtual alike) I may not know as well but whom I've decided I could shamelessly (if passively) flirt with using a workout pic here, a tasteful nude there. In that sense, "Close Friends" almost reads like a misnomer. Almost. For such erotic interactions depend on a kind of closeness, on a kind of flinty intimacy that has forced me to expand how it is I think about queer friendships between men. Friendships that make room for such sexually charged interactions and that allow an erotic porousness that feels refreshing for the way it actually exploits the very expansiveness of a figure as hazily sketched as a "close friend."

The queer elasticity of friendship (or, if we must rephrase it, the elasticity of queer friendship) is nothing new. The term *friend*— like *buddy* or *roommate*—has an extensive history of malleable use within the LGBTQ community: we are, let us not forget, not only "friends of Dorothy" but we've even adopted Garland-inspired jargon to refer to our best pals as our "Judys." In an April 1981 interview with the French magazine *Gai pied* titled "Friendship as a Way of Life," philosopher Michel Foucault actually put forth an even more provocative proposition about what we might think of as the inherent queerness *of* friendship. "Homosexuality," he pointed out, "is not a form of desire but something desirable"—a statement that, at the tail end of the twentieth century, still felt novel and radical. But he went one step further: "The development toward which the problem of homosexuality tends is the one of friendship." By that he meant that, unlike relationships between men and women, those between two men (and yes, he did only speak about men) had no template. "What would allow them to communicate?" he asked. "They face each other without terms or convenient words, with nothing to assure them about the meaning of the movement that carries them toward each other. They have to invent from A to Z, a relationship that is still formless, which is friendship: that is to say, the sum of everything through which they can give each other pleasure." Theirs would be (and is) uncharted territory. As Tom Roach further explained this century, the late philosopher's "work offers a powerful model for reimagining male friendship in particular. By jettisoning sexuality as the truth-telling fulcrum distinguishing friend from lover, it explodes the coercive and impoverishing codes of homosocial male bonding so crucial to patriarchal social hierarchies." If we dispense with the belief that friends and lovers are necessarily different categories (distinguishable because you'd have sex with one but not the other), then we could refashion the very social fabric we've become accustomed to.

This is the "way of life" that Foucault's interview nods toward. To be gay and to forge these new kinds of queered friendships would be a way to imagine a different world than the one we live in, away from the rigid ways in which we're called to relate to one another. In a way, Foucault was handily advancing a rather muted though not, for that, any less radical idea. Instead of insisting on an assimilationist take—wherein gay men would, for instance, merely aspire to achieve the social capital of the nuclear family, through coupledom and familial constructions—the French philosopher would rather have us reimagine the socially sanctioned relationships we are encouraged to value above all else. After all, the image of two adults moving toward a relationship in the search for sex is easily legible. "We must escape and help others to escape," he urges, "the readymade formulas of the pure sexual encounter and the lovers' fusion of identities." It makes sense that this would necessarily start with friendships, particularly with friendships that would allow for elements we've been encouraged to think of as exclusive to the lovers, to the couple, to the family.

Four decades after Foucault's musings, the 2021 culture issue of *T* magazine promised to offer, as its cover suggested, "a celebration of the relationships that helped us endure an impossible year." The issue, published the first spring since COVID-19 restrictions and lockdowns had brought the entire world to a standstill, was simply titled "With Friends." The headline was stylized as two words hastily handwritten on the page, as if encouraging us to see this topic as more casual, more intimate, than what would normally grace such a cover; it was also designed to accompany and complete a series of tableaus of all we do (sheltering, eating, working, etc.) with friends. In keeping with the issue's commitment to the very plurality of its organizing principle, readers were greeted with eight different covers, each of which illustrated many-varied versions of contemporary friendships: "Best Friends" (Chloë Sevigny and Natasha Lyonne hand in hand in a black-and-white candid pic); "Old Friends" (Rossy de Palma, Pedro Almodóvar, Antonio Banderas, and Penélope Cruz, all hugging each other close, dressed in Pedro's signature hot-red warm colors), "New Friends" (Rina Sawayama lying on a seated Elton John, the two holding hands), and so on and so forth.

In her introduction to the issue, editor Hanya Yanagihara explained that the impetus for this particular theme was a direct response to the ways in which 2020 had encouraged many to reassess the kinds of intimacies we treasured and nourished. The wide-ranging issue was an attempt not to codify but to catalog that most elastic of social relationships. "The quality that makes friendships singular—that they are the one serious relationship in our lives not bound by money or law—is also what makes them fragile," she wrote. "There are no rules about what a friendship can be: It needs only effort, and mutual commitment." That *only* is doing a lot of heavy lifting in that sentence—and not just because many other relationships in our lives similarly demand effort and mutual commitment (a therapist and a patient, say, but also, what are romantic partnerships without effort and mutual commitment?). But Yanagihara is right in suggesting friendships are singular:

there is no narrative template for them. Despite its ubiquity in our everyday social lives, it can sometimes feel like friendship is underappreciated—undervalued, even. There is no easy way to build a life around them, as Foucault would put it. That's mostly because "friendship" is in itself a nebulous concept, one as expansive as it is exhaustible. The word would seem to encompass, and thus flatten, such disparate relationships as schoolyard playmates and lifelong acquaintances, brunch buds and close confidants, not to mention everything in between. Friendships are sinuous and slippery. They can be short and intense or lifelong and comforting. They can stand in for tight support groups or branch out into broader coalitions. They can demand proximity or flourish in distance.

Yanagihara, of course, was no stranger to putting into words the dramatic intricacies of friendship. Her 2015 novel, *A Little Life*, could very well be described as an extended—if quite melodramatic—meditation on the vicissitudes of male friendships, their wounded and wounding scarring contours exactingly delineated with razor-sharp tenderness. As she wrote in that novel, ventriloquizing one of the many characters that populate her Boston- and New York City–set novel and echoing the words she'd use years later in her *T* magazine "With Friends" feature, "friendship was witnessing another's slow drip of miseries, and long bouts of boredom, and occasional triumphs. It was feeling honored by the privilege of getting to be present for another person's most dismal moments, and knowing that you could be dismal around him in return." The *him* is key, in sentence and novel. *A Little Life* is preternaturally concerned with male friendships: at its core are four young men who meet in a college dorm and whose friendships we witness blooming and ossifying, splintering and strengthening for decades to come. There's Willem, a guilelessly beautiful young waiter-slash-actor whose talents may outweigh his ambitions.

Malcolm, a promising Black architect from an affluent academic family in the Upper East Side. Jean Baptiste (JB), a visual artist of Haitian descent who's convinced he'll one day grace the pages of the art magazine he works at. And then there's Jude.

During the early sections of the book, which trace the ups and downs of the four boys' postcollege years, Jude is the book's most obliquely sketched character. All we learn about him comes from what scant facts his friends know about him. We know that he's an orphan. That he suffered some kind of accident that's left his legs quite badly damaged by the time he arrives at college. That he's brilliant at math and eventually at law. Oh, and that he's impossibly self-conscious despite having quite striking looks. Jude's aggressively traumatic past (which includes cruel brothers at a monastery, rampant sexual abuse, a life of child and later teenage sexual exploitation, and a string of violent events he has long learned to assuage by cutting his arms) is what eventually takes over the novel. But even as Yanagihara's prose thrusts itself into ever murkier territory as it conjures up new and increasingly disturbing episodes that operate as operatic riffs on darkly baroque fairy tales (with Jude constantly fending off famished hyenas or fleshy nameless beasts, figurations of his own past traumas and current curdling anxieties), the focus remains squarely on the elasticity of friendship. On the promising and yet terrifying emancipatory possibility that close friendships can proffer the likes of Jude.

Except the very concept *of* closeness is precisely what Yanagihara explodes in *A Little Life*. Speaking about her writing process, she told an interviewer that her interest in male friendships had to do with the limited emotional vocabulary men (regardless of their race, cultural affiliations, religion, or sexuality—and her protagonists do run the gamut in these regards) have. "One of the things I most enjoyed exploring," she shared, "is how these men's friendships, while close by anyone's definition, are also built upon a mutual desire to not truly know too much." This is most obvious in Jude, who guards his past, his body, even his needs and wants, with unsparing doggedness. Ever the keen if slightly cynical observer of a world he's convinced will never quite make room for him, a world so foreign to him he can only infiltrate it with carefully orchestrated performances of normalcy, Jude understands friendships as "a series of exchanges, of affections, of time, sometimes of money, always of information." To be someone's friend is to slowly, over time, get to know them better. But over the course of his life, Jude finds that close friends, *real* friends, will make room for ample accommodations that fall outside his narrow understanding of what it means to be a good friend.

The architecture of contemporary friendships (specifically male friendships, queer ones, really) is laid bare in the novel as infinitely pliable. Moreover, *A Little Life* champions visions of adulthood that do away with prescribed notions of what constitutes a well-lived life. The bonds these young men build with one another are presented as the most important ones they make in their lives; they exist almost as illustrative rebukes to what's expected, namely, those narratives about couples and families that, Willem and Jude, for instance, know to be more illusory than rewarding. "Why wasn't friendship as good as a relationship? Why wasn't it even better?" Willem asks himself early in the novel when he recognizes just how central his friends are to his own sense of self. He's the first to acknowledge how much Malcolm, JB, and Jude help contour the shape of his life. What he has with Jude, especially, the small domestic life the two shabbily first build for each other in the cramped and crappy apartment on Lispenard Street they rent together, opens him to wonder what one might get out of valuing friendship over any other social relationship: "It was two people who remained together, day after day, bound not by sex or physical attraction or money or children or property, but only by the shared agreement to keep going, the mutual dedication to a union that could never be codified." In Willem's words you can hear the very argument Yanagihara would put forth in *T* magazine all those years later. Friendship was nourishing and invigorating. But it was also enervating and enraging. This is why friendships can feel more expansive than romantic or familial relationships; the fact that they can't be easily described means they also can't be easily constrained or constricted. They can balloon out of your life with the swiftest of winds or they can grow heavy enough to anchor you to the ground.

What's long fascinated me about *A Little Life*, arguably one of the most hotly contested novels of the twenty-first century (seriously, any self-respecting gay man who's read it has *thoughts* on it), is how it captured the "problem" of homosexuality Foucault sketched all the way back in 1981. The porousness of love, erotic attraction, and friendship come to a head in the central coupling that eventually takes over the narrative. For it is Willem and Jude's relationship that ends up structuring the latter half of the novel. What begins as a college-aged codependent near-fraternal relationship—two orphaned boys clinging on to each other to build out a little life together—soon blooms (or warps, more like, depending on how you wish to understand such a transformation) into something that defies categorization. Forget a friendship that refuses to be codified (by the law, by familial traditions, by society at large). Their friendship becomes something rarer. Decades after first meeting Jude, the actor wakes up one day to find he's thinking of his very close friend in decidedly romantic ways. Actually, if he's honest with himself, he's looking at Jude in increasingly lustful ways. It's unclear to Willem whether this is a newfound realization a long time in the making or whether he's stumbled into a new way of looking at the one friend who gets him better than anyone else in his life, the person he's long bent his life around (to the detriment of past girlfriends). Theirs had always been a friendship built on care, on a childish way of moving through the world together with no worries about marriage or kids or family on their horizons. And so it remains once they decide to explore being a couple. Except, given Jude's past (and outright disdain for all things associated with sex), their relationship eventually twists itself into something that looks deceptively like a loving partnership despite it operating on rather strange and estranging circumstances.

In describing what they become—friends who love each other, lovers who don't make love—Willem again anticipates the word Yanagihara would later use in that *T* magazine issue: *singular.* Theirs is a relationship that's singular but workable. "He sometimes wondered," Yanigahara continues, "if it was simple lack of creativity—his and Jude's—that had made them both think that their relationship had to include sex at all." Of course, we could use just as descriptive if counterintuitive a moniker for it instead of *singular.* I would, at least; I would term it a *queer* kind of friendship. As Garth Greenwell puts it in a piece in *The Atlantic* that hailed *A Little Life* as the "Great Gay Novel" many had long been clamoring for, "The book vigorously defends friendship as a primary relationship, as central as marriage to the making of lives and communities." Its baroque illustration of trauma and suffering, archly allegorical as it may be, was anchored in an acute understanding that friendship was and remains central to the collective queer experience. That specific label may be ill suited to describe Jude and Willem (though the latter, an eventual famed award-winning actor, does eventually have to come out publicly even as he eschews any public association with the LGBTQ community). But there's no denying that, as Greenwell argues, Yanagihara had crafted a book rooted in a gay sensibility. It's not just that Jude and Willem eventually become an item or that JB openly identifies himself as a gay man. But that in exploring the nuances of what it means for men to care (and care for) other men in ways both romantic and sexual (and especially in ways that defy such a clear-cut dichotomy), A Little Life illustrates contemporary gay life in a decidedly modern way. "Just as Yanagihara's characters challenge conventional categories of gay identity, so A Little Life avoids the familiar narratives of gay fiction," Greenwell writes. The novel, he posits, is an operatic melodrama keyed into the same sensibility that has given us everything from Proust to Almodóvar. Here's where the very focus on a friendship that is modeled like a live-in romantic partnership, and yet does away with sex altogether, cannot help but be rooted in a queer understanding *of* friendship as a way of life Foucault was mapping out in the early 1980s. Jude and Willem all but demand that we redefine what we mean when we talk of them as lovers *and* as friends.

Moreover, within the pages of A Little Life Yanagihara places an astute chronicler of these kinds of relationships, an artist who becomes obsessed with his friends-as-muses. And who, as a kind of author stand-in, insists with his work on the importance of these bonds for himself and for the greater audience he eventually reaches. JB's portraiture, in fact, becomes the most obvious way in which Yanagihara posits friendship as a relationship worth exploring artistically. The young artist's first showing is titled The Boys. Publicly displaying the series of twenty-four paintings based on photographs he'd taken of Willem, Malcolm, and Jude is, coincidentally, the moment when his and Jude's friendship first fractures: just as JB manages to exalt his love for his friends, he loses one by failing to adhere to the very tenets of that friendship. While JB finds inspiration in Malcolm and Willem, it is Jude whom he's most taken with. His fascination with Jude's face and his body, with the striking way his eyes catch the light and the arresting way he moves through the world, leads JB to constantly experiment with his own brushstrokes and color palettes to better capture his friend's wayward self-consciousness, and the beauty to be found therein. Such a fascination is ultimately what leads JB to create some of his most accomplished works. That is precisely the case in *The Boys*, where two Jude paintings (*Jude with Cigarette* and *Jude After Sickness*, both created without his friend's consent) are, everyone agrees, the best in the show. These portraits wound Jude immensely. Not just because of the way JB had crossed a line but because they'd forced him to reckon with how others—how strangers—could and had seen him.

This is what friends do so well. To have a close friend is to allow yourself to be seen, to be known, two things Jude had long associated with being made vulnerable, being made unsafe. More than his other friends, Jude understands the unwanted violence of an artist's piercing gaze. And every time he comes across a sketch of himself at JB's hand, Jude cannot help but bristle at the unguarded nakedness he experiences under his friend's probing (if loving) gaze. Unlike the openness, say, of one Frank O'Hara gleefully posing naked for his friends (something JB always wanted Jude to do), Jude finds himself becoming a begrudging muse. He's at the center of most of JB's shows, which end up inadvertently chronicling his life for decades to come, first as an individual and later as half of a couple. For it is JB who most trenchantly offers an outside commentary on the coupling of Willem and Jude, a pairing the artist kindly resents because he had tender (perhaps even lustful) feelings for both of his friends. You can see it in his devoted attention to both of their faces, their bodies, their lives. And he is the one who most accurately clocks them. The night when the two have him over at their apartment on Green Street to let him know they've been quietly dating for quite some time, JB reaches for an art reference that's meant to be cutting but that also captures the honeyed domesticity that had always defined their relationship: "Watching you two in the kitchen is like watching a slightly more racially ambiguous version of that John Currin painting," he tells them. He's referring to Currin's oil work *Homemade Pasta* (1999). In it, two men, one in a red-and-white checkered apron, the other in a tan one, are helping each other extrude noodles. They're all smiles, suggesting a blissful contentment in each other's presence and their shared domestic space. With its warm colors and hazy edges, Currin's portrait offers a clichéd image of 1950s coziness, one here reframed with two men. But it's quite a neutered vision of homely intimacy—precisely what Jude and Willem have built for themselves ever since they first shared an apartment after graduation on Lispenard Street. Here's an image of a same-sex couple as a partnership devoid of any hint of sex, which serves as a preamble to how JB himself will later portray his two friends in a show wholly devoted to them: *Frog and Toad*.

The nod to Arnold Lobel's beloved illustrated books is not lost on Yanagihara's readers—many of whom cannot now approach Frog and Toad without the queered iconicity they've come to embody. Lobel first published *Frog and Toad Are Friends* in 1970. The slim volume, which he also illustrated, consisted of five stories centered on a tall happy-go-lucky green frog and a sometimes-dour stout brown toad. Their everyday adventures focused, in that first volume, on their anchored friendship. In one, for instance, Toad bemoans the fact that he never gets any mail. It's why the afternoons find him rather forlorn: "This is my sad time of day," he tells Frog. It's sad because no one writes to him. And so, to cheer up his friend, Frog runs back to his place and quickly jots down a letter to Toad. It reads, quite simply: "Dear Toad, I am glad that you are my best friend. Your best friend, Frog." The narrative is delightfully simple: a celebration of the small gestures we can nudge ourselves to do for one another. So small that they feel all the more remarkable for the way they can affect our friends. This is friendship as care. Elsewhere, Frog eggs on Toad to stop his hibernating and enjoy the pleasures of spring, helps Toad look for a missing button for his jacket, and even helps distract him while Toad is sick in bed.

It makes sense why JB looked to Lobel (as he had to Currin) to make sense of his friends-turned-couple. Mostly because Frog and Toad operate as a liminal representation of a friendship that may well be more but that is, also, oddly lacking in sexual chemistry. As *The New York Times* theater critic Jesse Green put it in a piece about "The Gay History of America's Classic Children's Books," the Frog and Toad book series isn't gay-themed. "But it's not *not* gay-themed either . . . Lobel is careful to make Frog and Toad entirely nonsexual," he adds. "They sleep apart, and Toad even dons a modest Edwardian bathing suit when he swims. Instead of innate animal passion, they model the elements of love that have to be discovered and cultivated: companionship, compromise, acceptance, good humor. They get into scrapes separately but get out of them together, which is not a bad definition of marriage." But that's also not a definition exclusive to marriage. The tension at the heart of understanding Frog and Toad as queer avatars, as a thinly veiled same-sex couple (that spoke to Lobel's own homosexuality, which has become central to his legacy in the years since his passing in 1987 after living with AIDS for some years), stems from the schism that presumably exists between "close friends" and "life partners." And once you've evacuated sex from the equation, when, as Lobel does, you've made such a relationship "entirely nonsexual," we're left with very few words that would helpfully describe what Frog and Toad are to each other without resorting to, as Green does,

more readily legible concepts. But this stems from a lack of imagination, in Willem's assessment: "The word 'friend' was so vague, so
undescriptive and unsatisfying—how could he use the same term to
describe what Jude was to him that he used for India or the Henry
Youngs? And so they had chosen another, more familiar form of
relationship, one that hadn't worked. But now they were inventing
their own type of relationship, one that wasn't officially recognized
by history or immortalized in poetry or song, but which felt truer
and less constraining."

When I first read *A Little Life*, in the summer of 2015, when you
couldn't board a subway train in New York City without seeing Peter Hujar's *Orgasmic Man* photo staring out at you from the book's
famed cover, I was thinking a lot about how my own marriage—to
a "best friend you can have sex with"—felt legible because of how
neutered it was. I was starting to wonder whether I could not also
make room for other (better? closer?) friends I could have sex with.
The kind that would help me break out of the rote familiarity I'd
found myself in. It's no surprise I sought that in artist friends who
felt more unshackled from notions of normalcy and propriety, and
who exploded how I could envision not just such intimacies but
perhaps my own worldview. For, as Hua Hsu opens a *New Yorker*
article on Jacques Derrida's *The Politics of Friendship*, "Stories about
love offer models for how you might commit your life to another
person. Stories about friendship are usually about how you might
commit to life itself." Except such a dichotomy feels, if not incom-
plete, at least intentionally parochial. As Hsu helpfully explains,
the Algerian-born French philosopher is best remembered for the
way he attacked the very notion *of* dichotomy (this was the promise of deconstruction as a philosophical inquiry): "Derrida wanted
to disrupt our drive to generate meaning through dichotomies,"
Hsu writes. "These seeming opposites were mutually constitutive,

he pointed out: just because one concept prevailed over the other didn't mean that either was stable or self-defined." In thinking about *A Little Life* and even the Frog and Toad books, stories about friendship are not easily discerned from stories about romance. More to the point, what kind of disservice might we be doing to ourselves when we pit love and friendship against each other? Couldn't we deconstruct this dichotomy to better show how they could be self-engendering instead?

Here's where Foucault, whose own queerness necessarily seeps into his life philosophy, may be more helpful than Derrida. For at the heart of Foucault's meditations on queer friendships was a key question: "How is it possible for men to be together? To live together, to share their time, their meals, their room, their leisure, their grief, their knowledge, their confidences?" This is precisely what Willem and Jude find themselves illustrating, why JB so accurately reads them as a version of Frog and Toad. Theirs is a friendship that defies easy categorization. They are friends *and* lovers. But also friends *and not* lovers. In a way, by their inability to put sex at the heart of their partnership, they accomplish an instantiation of what Foucault was getting at in *Gai pied*. When he asked, "What is to be 'naked' among men, outside of institutional relations, family, profession, and obligatory camaraderie?" he was obviously being literal and yet not (ergo the quotation marks).

This is a question that continues to be posed decades since: How can we build and acknowledge relationships that straddle the line between the romantic and the erotic without carefully delineating the boundary that distinguishes them? Might we expand our notion of "love" or make room for more exhaustive visions of the erotic? For bell hooks, the answer lies in asking those very questions. Rather than accept the erotic as being displaced solely onto the world of the couple, onto the realm of the lover (and away, say, from the geography of the friend), hooks calls us to embrace the erotic pull all around us. It's why she quotes Frank Browning, who insists on forging and privileging the erotic in our everyday lives: "By erotic," he writes, "I mean all the powerful attractions we might have: for mentoring and being mentored, for unrealizable flirtation, for intellectual tripping, for sweaty mateship at play or at work, for spiritual ecstasy, for being held in silent grief, for explosive rage at a common enemy, for the sublime love of friendship." Following his thinking, hooks sees a powerful invitation to imagine a fuller sense of possibility in how we interact with others.

Just as we can conceptualize the chaste friendships of Lobel and Yanagihara as queered attempts to expand what we can find in those who most intimately know us, the flip side would require us to lust after those very friends in decidedly nonthreatening ways. There lay the porousness of a "close friend," an expansive relational category that flirts with erotic potential while refusing its totalizing force. We would all do better to nurture such close friendships, as erotic or as chaste as they may be, without fearing them becoming something else. "Patriarchy," hooks writes, "has sought to repress and tame erotic passion precisely because of its power to draw us into greater and greater communion with ourselves, with those we know most intimately, and," crucially, she adds, "with the stranger."

7.

TWO'S COMPANY

I GOT MARRIED FIVE MONTHS SHY OF MY THIRTY-SECOND birthday. It was a small ceremony at city hall in New York City, with only our closest family members in attendance. We wanted a marriage, cared little for a wedding. *Wanted* is perhaps too strong a word. Our decision to marry was driven by purely practical purposes. Just as there would be no fanciful celebration at some restored barn where guests would take Polaroids against a backdrop adorned with a hashtag boasting our names, there had been no wildly romantic down-on-one-knee proposal. Instead, we'd arrived at the decision to marry the same way my partner and I had made plenty of other decisions about our life together: calmly discussing it over dinner. Spurred as it was by a looming change in my immigration status (my student visa had served its purpose and would be expiring soon), we'd opted to get married as a way to solve a practical problem. A marriage—and the prospect of the green card that would swiftly come with it—was a solution that felt obvious. We already lived together. Had done so for years. We'd met each other's families and had discussed, briefly, though in no uncertain terms, how little either of us cared for starting a family of our own. For all intents and purposes, we led quite the domestic life together already. A signature and some vows wouldn't alter much. Nothing would really change between us. Sure, we'd come to wear wedding rings (simple bands ordered online) and would have proof of it in a piece of paper (helpful in various bureaucratic contexts), but the marriage certificate felt more like a formality about what our relationship already meant to ourselves.

Would I have felt differently about marriage (about my wedding, actually) if I hadn't come from what we've euphemistically come to call a "broken family"? Could my parents' divorce when I was young really have so stunted me to think I needed to disavow the pretense of the happily ever after offered by that straightest of rituals? Might I, in another life, with another partner, have found it exhilarating to get a proper proposal and daydream, perhaps, of a giant wedding where I'd be convinced my life would irrevocably be changed thereafter? Was my practicality merely proof that such civil rights (federally gained for couples like us only the year before, mind you) could become white noise to our life together?

Such rhetorical questions make for great therapy session fodder. But they remain wildly impractical for everyday conversations. My cool disaffection regarding marriage and what it would entail, what it would say about me, about us, about our values and our desires, was, I think, symptomatic of how distrustful I felt of the narratives around it. Here I do have my mother to thank. After separating from my dad, she rebuked any talk of marriage. Even (or especially, really) though she's lived with her decades-long boyfriend for longer now than she was ever married to my father. The brutal pragmatism with which I approached my own marriage felt in line with how she'd modeled her own long-term relationship: I would marry if I must, but with a cynical eye to its instrumentality. For years, it helped that such an image, such a happy ending, was but a pipe dream. One couched in words like *civil unions* and *domestic partnerships*, in makeshift simulations of the *real thing*. There were no rom-coms that ended with two men getting married. No marriage plots that concluded with same-sex wedded bliss. No telenovela finales that found gay couples walking down the aisle. Long reduced to living outside of such romantic plots (as many of us queer kids from divorced homes tend to do), I'd convinced myself that to buy into such narratives was naive at best and insidious at worst. Such cynicism had served me well in undergraduate queer theory classes and in erudite grad school seminars about structuralism. Even now, with my own divorce squarely in the rearview mirror, I've come to wonder whether such cynicism may well hold the key to why marriage in the twenty-first century remains such a contested and ill-fitting social contract.

At its most elemental, marriage is the most well-known architecture of intimacy. Beyond the pomp and circumstance of the wedding, the very premise of a marriage is a way to give shape—give meaning, even—to a relationship. Legally, most obviously. But in even more mundane ways. There's an arc to a marriage, one that's made legible to those around you. You wear rings to remind others, as much as yourself, of who and what you're devoted to. In this sense, marriage remains (barring adoption, say) the most socially sanctioned way to create familial bonds. You don't need to have studied J. L. Austin via Judith Butler to understand that marital vows create a new reality by their very utterance. "I do" and "I take thee" and "I now pronounce you" all have a way of turning a boyfriend into a husband, a once-stranger into kin. It's a kind of magic trick that rightfully dazzles so many couples and families alike.

What most of us want—what I craved, I can see now in the relationship that led me down the metaphorical aisle—is

companionship. Company, in fact. For isn't that what we're promised will be found (*only*) in coupledom, (*only*) in marriage? Or, as
Stephen Sondheim put it in the title song for his 1970 collaboration
with George Furth, *Company*: Isn't that what it's really about? It's
true, whenever I find myself thinking about the promises and perils
of getting married (today), or the ways I am sorry-grateful for my
years as a happily married man, I can't help but stumble onto lyrics
and aphorisms and dialogue and punch lines from that Sondheim
classic. The Tony-winning "concept musical" remains, in my eyes,
the most probing examination of the very concept *of* marriage. Neither sunnily optimistic about what men and women find in long-
term relationships nor woefully despondent about what one loses
in such partnerships, *Company* is, like the very best of Sondheim,
awash in ambiguities, reminding us instead that we all live in a
world where uncertainty is the only thing we can ever be certain of.

Ahead of the show's Broadway premiere at the Alvin Theatre
in April 1970, Sondheim described the musical as being about "how
difficult it is to be married and how much more difficult it is not
to be married." Ostensibly taking place during a surprise birthday
party for Robert (Bobby), *Company* evades such a neat characteri-
zation. Looking back on this abstract musical, Sondheim wrote that
"the show takes place not over a period of time, but in an instant
in Robert's mind, perhaps on a psychiatrist's couch, perhaps at
the moment when he comes into his apartment on his thirty-fifth
birthday." There is no plot here, marriage or otherwise, just staged
interactions between Bobby and his married friends (and three of
his girlfriends) that by sheer force of accretion highlight the plight of
the married and the unmarried. While Bobby is greeted by friends
and a birthday cake during the show's opening number ("Company"), the scenes that follow function as echoed memories and
daydreamed scenarios that bleed in and out of his consciousness

and into each other. There is a kaleidoscopic structure to this ambitious theater piece.

With every new scene, the lives of those (ostensibly) happily married, and those (presumably) happily not, are constantly juxtaposed. In one, for instance, you witness the avowed bachelor visiting with Sarah and her husband, Harry, only to have their interaction be intercut with a song that serves as commentary. "The Little Things You Do Together" is ostensibly about Sarah and Harry's prickly, bickering intimacy, but sung by a character squarely outside the action happening onstage, the lyrics highlight well-worn domestic contentment: it's the little things (like the concerts you enjoy together or the children you destroy together) that keep marriages intact, as we're told. Later, as Bobby talks to his friends Peter and Susan about the three girls he's been seeing, those eligible bachelorettes do a song and dance about how he isn't really ready to settle down with any one of them ("You Could Drive a Person Crazy"). In such a dichotomy, the musical voiced contemporary anxieties about the very purpose of marriage as an institution in a post-sixties world. The April 1970 issue of *Playboy* magazine, published just as Broadway audiences were first seeing the Hal Prince–directed and Michael Bennet–choreographed production of *Company*, feels like proof that there was something in the ether gnawing away at the sanctity of marriage. In "Playboy's Party Jokes," one humorous setup gestured toward swingers: "Our Unabashed Dictionary defines *suburb* as a community where a man will lend you his wife but not his golf clubs." Meanwhile a letter from Oak Ridge, Tennessee, (name withheld by request) exalted the joys of "wife swapping" that begins by praising the practice for the way it increased the couple's enjoyment in each other but ends up striking a chord that goes beyond sex: "All married people," the letter writer states, "have feelings of various intensities for others:

for their children, their job, their in-laws, their dog, etc. Sexual relations (or *any* relations) with others that do not endanger or encroach upon the marriage are not immoral." It's in that parenthetical that we can read a more expansive vision of marriage than the one normally peddled—that idea that your other half (and *only* your other half) completes you.

In a substantive conversation with "the first lady of sex education," Mary Steichen Calderone, the former head of the Sex Information and Education Council of the United States (SIECUS), founded in 1964, is asked about the merits of "extramarital sex" and of the radical possibilities of "communal marriages." *Playboy* readers, the interview suggests, would be curious about these seemingly vanguard ideas about contemporary intimacies. But she does present a persuasive argument for the need to expand how we relate to one another, and how to break free from society's strict strictures about how we negotiate our intimate relationships—particularly when it comes to marriage, which has reduced a more expansive social and familial structure into a mere unit of two. She thinks these developments suggest people are eager to relate to one another in groups. People are seeking more contact with those outside of their family unit, she argues. "They are rebelling against the loneliness of the urban nuclear family, in which a mother, a father and a few children have only one another for emotional support. Perhaps society is trying to reorganize itself to satisfy these yearnings."

Company's arrival on Broadway in 1970 addressed questions about the necessity, let alone urgency, of getting married that had been percolating in mainstream U.S. culture in the preceding decades. As Stephanie Coontz notes in her exhaustive *Marriage, a History* study, the late 1950s and 1960s gave way to an onslaught of critiques (feminist and otherwise) that began eroding what, in our imagination, remains the picket-fenced picture-perfect version of postwar marital bliss. "By the late 1970s," Coontz writes, changes in legislation (including the *Loving v. Virginia* and *Roe v. Wade* rulings) and in the women's rights movement (including the pill and consciousness-raising groups) "had merged to produce an enormous change in people's attitudes toward personal relationships. Surveys from the late 1950s to the end of the 1970s found a huge drop in support for conformity to social roles and a much greater focus on self-fulfillment, intimacy, fairness, and emotional gratification." Amid these cultural shifts, Betty Friedan would single out "the problem that has no name" with regards to suburban housewives in 1963's *The Feminine Mystique*, while Robert Lindner's *Must You Conform?* (1955) and John Keats's *The Crack in the Picture Window* (1956) had men wondering whether their prescribed roles weren't jail sentences of their own.

A full decade before *Company* would dissect marriage from the outside, Richard Yates's marital melodrama *Revolutionary Road* had stirred up plenty of controversy regarding its cynical illustration of a doomed suburban couple. So much so that its author eventually had to come out in defense of his novel, asking decades later, "Who but a maniac or a goddamn fool would sit down and write a novel attacking marriage? And who'd want to read such a novel?" (Many of us, Yates, I assure you.)

Yates's couple offered a portrait of the dark underbelly of the bright postwar promise of the suburbs. Neat lawns, white picket fences, and picture windows suggest a comforting sense of order but also an orderly sense of conformity. Baffled by having turned into what they'd once decried, Frank and April Wheeler start to look at their house up on Revolutionary Road less like an idyllic home and more like a well-manicured prison. The tragic story of the Wheelers, a couple who see themselves trapped in their 1950s picture-perfect home, lends itself to being read as an indictment of an insidious type of conformity that postwar (white) suburban married life epitomized—the kind Friedan, Lindner, and Keats had diagnosed in their own contemporaneous work. As critic Alfred Kazin put it, *Revolutionary Road* "locates the new American tragedy squarely on the field of marriage." That was such a ringing endorsement, or offered such a titillating promise, that Yates's publisher, Little, Brown, decided to use Kazin's blurb on the book's jacket cover.

Despite Yates's protestations, there is plenty of ammunition in *Revolutionary Road* if one were to launch an attack on the nuclear family's central bond. Frank and April Wheeler—whom everyone they know, including themselves, agrees were once very special people destined for great things—have calcified into a simulacrum of what a well-adjusted married couple should look like in the mid-1950s. The novel is a story about how their relationship and the many compromises they've made to maintain it have crippled them, stunting the potential they once had. Frank, like a model dutiful husband, begrudgingly ends up taking a job at the same company his old man used to work at while April, leaving behind any ambitions of becoming an actress, hones her homemaking skills. April's performance as devoted wife and mother strains her every waking moment; it's no surprise she's most brutally honest when she allows herself to disown those very limiting roles. After convincing Frank they should pack up and leave for Paris ("People are alive there!"), finally taking the reins of a life long hijacked by compromises, she eases into a more relaxed mode that comforts and scares Frank in equal measure. That's because, as he slowly finds out, he too has been living under a guise he worries he may not be able to live without. Whether seducing Maureen, a young secretary at work, or recounting a wartime anecdote to friends Shep and Milly Campbell, Frank's every move is shown to be painfully calculated. He's most alive when performing a bolder, smarter, more worldly version of himself. But where his young conquest and his all-too-nice neighbors are all happy to play along and indulge Frank's posturing, April is an uncaring audience. Therein lies the true tragedy of the Wheelers; they may have both been born for the spotlight, but while she's eager to try on new roles, he's too self-absorbed to see how stale his own performance has gotten.

The novel's bleak outlook on marriage as an institution (Yates's posturing aside)—not to mention its tragic end, which finds April bleeding out following a botched abortion—is no doubt what kept *Revolutionary Road* from hitting the big screen for close to fifty years. Sam Mendes, who'd already tackled the thorny broken promises of marriage in both a Donmar Warehouse production of *Company* in 1995 (for which he won a Laurence Olivier Award) and in his feature film debut, the suburbia-set *American Beauty*, in 1999 (for which he won an Academy Award), brought Yates's book to the screen, reuniting in the process, his then wife, Kate Winslet, with her *Titanic* costar Leonardo DiCaprio. Mendes zeroed in on the tragedy of the Wheelers as speaking to a broader theme that, despite its postwar trappings, would appeal to contemporary audiences. "The more I read the book I realized it's not a novel about suburbia, it's a novel about men and women," he told *The Believer*. "It seemed to me just to be about that very specific moment when you realize that you're not living the life you wanted and how that is universal." Calling it his most intimate yet, Mendes produced a film about intimacy itself—about what happens when you become estranged both from the person you once were (and could be) and from the one you're living next to. But is that the lesson to be learned about the Wheelers or about marriage writ large? After all, such a message is all over *Company*, which is populated by couples who have, to varying degrees of success, resigned themselves to a world in which their own marriages have soured, where their settling down has become indistinguishable from merely and begrudgingly settling.

April and Frank exist on the page and on the screen as fleshed-out illustrations of the immense chasm that exists between what could be and what is, one made all the murkier when you're wedded to the very institution that would have you ignore such complaints. Their tragedy proceeds from being unable to imagine, and later still unable to make happen, any alternative from the life they've chosen to live. The first glimpse we get of April in the film is from her soon-to-be-husband's perspective; it announces her as a "first-rate" girl with the world at her fingertips. The establishing shots of New York's moonlit cityscape place us in a West Village house party throbbing with beautiful guests, where a youthful Frank is struck dumb by the sight before him. Amid the crowd is a blond girl in a little black dress. Unaware she's being watched, April has a drink in one hand and a cigarette in the other. Our eyes, like Frank's no doubt, are drawn to her red lips as she exhales, then at her eyes as she fixes her stare on us. Here is a girl, as Yates's narrator informs us, "whose every glance and gesture could make [Frank's] throat fill up with longing." The playfully pretentious flirtation that follows ("What are you interested in?" April asks; "Honey—if I had the answer to that one, I bet I'd bore us both to death in half an hour," Frank quips) fades as Mendes closes in on the anguished face of a slightly older Frank, sitting in the audience while his wife holds back tears as she takes a bow. The local production of Robert E. Sherwood's 1935 play *The Petrified Forest* has been a disaster and, as the chatty old lady behind Frank tells her friend, April in the lead role of Gabby "was very disappointing." In a flash, the glimmer of possibility of that sunny couple has soured into a stunted simulacrum of happiness. The need to conform, to be "just like everybody else," has stifled them both. Far from being the revelation onstage she once hoped she'd be ("despite the heavy make-up," Yates tells us, "you could see the warmth of humiliation rising in her face and neck"), her embarrassing stint as Gabby, in front of her neighbors, reminds her she is no better than the suburban performers around her. What follows is a tragic tale of a husband and a wife unable to navigate such a quiet failure without seeing in it a larger lesson about how whatever promise they once had is now irrevocably gone.

This is the same animating fear one can read in Bobby's reticence in *Company* toward finding a girl and settling down—even as the many friends who keep him company insist there's more to their marriages than what he can see. It's much better living it than looking at it, he's told. But it's not just Bobby. In the show's most technically difficult song ("Getting Married Today"), we witness his friend Amy voicing every single anxious thought any would-be bride could have about the prospect of finally getting hitched. The scene, which tees up the end of act 1, finds Amy in her wedding gown having an exhausting case of last-minute jitters. Her groom-to-be Paul is all too happy to celebrate Amy on this day, excited to begin their life together. He's the definition of a supportive partner, calm, cool, and collected even on this most hectic of days. All while his would-be-wife is spiraling, singing not just about her shrink and suicide notes but about more concrete concerns about what a wedding may do to their relationship. Calling a wedding a prehistoric ritual and noting that *fidelity* may be the most horrifying word she's ever heard, Amy runs through plenty of angst-inducing thoughts ahead of her wedding ceremony. She fears both Paul and herself would be ruining their lives by losing their identities. So, thanks a bunch, she tells those gathered for her wedding, but she's most definitely *not* getting married today. That bleak sketch of a marriage, and the anxieties it's rooted in, was and remains a cliché. In many ways, Amy is pulling from the very imagery Yates (and later

Mendes) was sketching, this idea that marriage can only ever sour a relationship, can only further erode one's sense of self. But that is here both highlighted and neutered by the fanciful comedy that encases its delivery; Amy's increasingly deranged patter is played up against operatic interludes that call up traditional wedding songs— all while Paul sings modestly and earnestly about the love he has for his soon-to-be-wife. Truly, there is no funnier number in *Company* than "Getting Married Today" and similarly none so heartfelt. Curiously, it is only once Bobby proposes to Amy in a momentary fit of ill-thought-out boldness that Amy comes to her senses and opts to go through with the wedding as planned.

The year *Revolutionary Road* arrived on screens was the same year audiences in the United States were treated to a filmed performance of *Company*, broadcast as part of the thirty-fifth season of *Great Performances* on PBS. The 2008 revival of the show, developed and directed by John Doyle, was my first encounter with the show itself. I still own the DVD I bought soon after it came out, so mesmerized was I by this Raúl Esparza–fronted reimagining of Sondheim and Furth's creation. With no attempt to locate the action as a period piece nor to anchor it in the contemporary present, Doyle opted instead to abstract it even further than director Hal Prince had in the original production. Long gone was a set that captured the sheer urbanity of New York City (what Clive Barnes's review in *The New York Times* had described as "a mixture between an East Side multiplex, Alcatraz and an exhibition display of some 20 years ago demonstrating the versatility of elevators"; yes, the original show had actual working elevators onstage!). Instead, Doyle stripped the stage bare. All that adorned it was a grand piano, a white column with a radiator at its base, and various clear cubes that doubled as every kind of furniture piece the numbers called for. He also did away with the orchestra, making his cast a true self-contained "company" where every member of the ensemble (barring Bobby, who only sits down at the piano in the final number) plays one or various instruments throughout the show. With such a seemingly cerebral conceit, one that took *Company*'s subtext and played it up onstage, Doyle highlighted the alienating feelings Bobby wrestles with throughout. Moreover, in refusing the naturalism that would otherwise anchor the show, Doyle stressed a defamiliarizing conceit (upping the Brechtian influence Sondheim had toyed with in his music and lyrics). What this left us with, and what's even easier to recognize in the *Great Performances* recording, is the lack of intimacy between its players, the way *Company*'s many couples find (or lose their) closeness in distance. Sarah and Harry's karate demonstration finds them on opposite ends of the stage, not touching at all; Bobby's sexual encounter with flight attendant April is similarly touch-free as the two characters merely circle around and caress the piano. Moreover, given that much of the stage is shrouded in darkness and many of the ensemble wears dark blue or all black, with spotlights punctuating their placement on the stage, Doyle's *Company* almost has the effect of feeling like a radio play about alienation.

"If you're afraid of loneliness, don't marry." The oft-quoted line comes from Russian playwright Anton Chekhov. From his diaries, in fact. And for Sondheim, it captured the very essence of what he and Furth wanted to convey with *Company*. It's that portrait of loneliness that Yates so carefully had sketched with his own April. Mrs. Frank Wheeler (arguably a role the once promising young woman never saw herself being reduced to) lives with a constant sense that she's not just lonely but alone in the world—even when such loneliness comes from the inescapable presence of her husband. It's why, while she may not be a revelation of an actress on the stage, she's a consummate performer in her daily life. Her smiles are always tentative, on the verge of cracking open a well of tears, whether in anger, sadness, or quite possibly both. For if there's one thing Yates perfectly captures about married life, whether in times of marital bliss or misery, it is the way marriage forces you to live with an ever-present witness. Only one that can exacerbate one's loneliness. Forcing you to face another every morning necessarily affects how you present yourself. For some, this becomes emboldening, getting you to live up to the best version of yourself, as seen in another person's eyes. For others, it becomes a burden, where one's daily life starts to depend on quickly changing performances that attempt to hide a person you're sure your partner won't ever tolerate. This is what makes the Wheelers' marriage so ripe for dissection; when they look at each other, they have a hard time untangling their respective posturings from the real thing. They may as well be looking at each other from opposite ends of a spotlit stage singing out their grievances with no suggestion they'd hear, let alone understand, what they're voicing. In their grown familiarity, they've become strangers.

Yates was defensive about tacking onto the Wheelers the weight of marriage writ large, but *Revolutionary Road*, both on the page and on the screen, is a study in how commitment and compromise can chip away at our own individuality. What was once a promising possibility (oh the people we could be with and for each other!) can stiffen and stifle you if you're not careful. Or if you're careless. To be married is to constantly have to acknowledge another, both as witness and as partner. The emotional work that entails, and in particular the need to perform for each other, is what asphyxiates April and what eventually leads Frank to find solace in someone else's bed. The Wheelers become a cautionary tale, a reminder that traditional institutions offer nothing more than rigid templates. April and Frank are stuck performing roles they long wish they

could've shed, roles that restrict them from breaking out of the re-
straints of the traditional marriage institution: he the breadwinner,
she the homemaker. If only we were more open with one another
and allowed for different configurations—of desire, of success—we
might be able to break through the traditions of which April and
Frank's unhappiness is so symptomatic.

All of those discussions, of course, assume a centrality to marriage as an institution. Even *Company*, which has now spurred decades' worth of discussions as to whether Bobby's final song, "Being
Alive," presents a rosy vision of marriage or outright disavows its
very construct, cannot escape its hold as *the* way in which adults
are called to assess their own personal development. A marriage is
a milestone. But it is also an end point. It's why, in Sondheim's eyes,
Company is a show about the hardships of being married and how
harder it is to be unmarried.

In a persuasive reading of Sondheim's approach to these
themes, critic Kay Young posits that the composer and lyricist was
always wary of endings (of the possibility *of* endings, really). A consummate student of musical theater history, Sondheim had grown
up studying the intricate narrative and melodic possibilities of this
most American of genres—especially in works like *Carousel*, *The
King and I*, and *Oklahoma!*, all of which structured their endings
around happy weddings. Marriage was *the* ending in musical theater and Sondheim spent the better part of his career deconstruct-
ing the conflation between those musical ends and those marital
beginnings. In refusing the happy ending that musical comedy had
long depended on, Sondheim pushed the genre to better know itself. In his work, there is no illusion about marriage setting up a
happily ever after. Or, as Young puts it, "Love and marriage, as the
ends in an aesthetic which normally carry with them the discovery
of meaning and truth from out of the chaos which is life, become

themselves the chaos, or just small moments which interact with other small moments that when taken collectively compose a life."

It explains why Sondheim, Furth, and Prince so struggled with landing an apt closer for the show. During their Boston try-out, Sondheim wrote a song titled "Happily Ever After." While some lyrics from that tune would eventually bleed into the eventual closer, "Being Alive," the tone, musically and lyrically, is much more dour in "Happily Ever After." Disavowing the promise of its title, the song paints a depressing vision of marriage, one full of unfathomable compromises and hopeless feelings. The song was so bleak the director realized it couldn't well be left in the show lest the audience exit the theater not just in tears but questioning their very existence. "If I heard that song I wouldn't get married for anything in the whole world," Prince recalled. He promptly asked Sondheim to write a more uplifting song, though the composer knew it would need to be laced with something else. "A sudden positive song, one without irony, would be unearned and pandering," Sondheim argued, "not to mention monotonous, since there would be only one thing to say: namely, marriage is wonderful."

What's remarkable is the way the irony *in* "Being Alive" is tempered not (solely) by the lyrics but by the way the song repurposes the choral asides that punctuate the show's opening number. This is why "Being Alive" hits differently when performed within the context of the show and when it's sung, say, by a performer at a concert or a cabaret (or an audition or a Broadway album or by a character in a Noah Baumbach film about divorce titled *Marriage Story*, say). There's a twinge of wry sadness throughout the song that's hard to shake off without the scattered assurances Bobby's friends lob at him (and us) throughout. He's told it's much better to live in it rather than to look at it, and to avoid fearing it won't be perfect. Such invocations lessen the wry, despondent tone the song can otherwise take. Though, ultimately, his final lyrics—where he sings that alone is not alive—and the image of an inscrutable smile adorning Bobby's face lend the show's ending an ambiguous sense of closure that, in turn, has made it into a kind of Rorschach test for however it is you may feel about its central themes.

At its heart, *Company* is a musical about how Bobby remains a stranger to and estranged from those closest to him, whom he's perhaps unwittingly content to keep at bay. As spectral spectator to his friends' jointly lived lives, Bobby is (or has been, in most iterations of the Tony-winning piece) a cipher whose distance from the intimacies he's in such close proximity to allows him to serve as the audience's surrogate, an ambling presence that keeps us wondering whether marriage really is all that. He's also always been, well, you know. Or maybe you don't. Maybe that's part of the point. Or beside it. But ever since the show opened, questions about Bobby's sexual and romantic inclinations have followed—tinging every reading of the show and its sexual politics with a queerness that's hard to avoid. Mainly because it feels like it's *the* point. Who better, after all, to mount a cutting and cutthroat appraisal of the heteronormative marriage structure and of the intimacies such strictures allow but an eligible gay bachelor unwilling to be tied down?

Even though such whispers have followed *Company* from its very start, Sondheim and Furth, both gay men themselves, long voiced denials of such a reading of the show. In his rather mixed review, the first of several to run in *The New York Times*, theater critic Clive Barnes added an aside that both opened and shut down such gossip about *Company*'s central lead: "In case you have any doubts about his sexual inclination—and I am not sure that I did," he writes, Bobby has "three girlfriends on the side." The parenthetical, not to mention the entire sentence, only makes sense if it's answering a question Barnes imagines other audience members asking themselves. (*Variety*, in a much more scathing review on the Boston tryout, went one further: "As it stands now," the piece read, the show is "for ladies' matinees, homos and misogynists.") Beyond what's on the page (and on the stage), *Company*'s Bobby has flirted with such queer readings for reasons that seem obvious on the one hand (here is an urbane, witty bachelor who has no desire to live the life of conformity his married friends lead) and more metatextual on the other (Sondheim's eventual lover, *Psycho*'s very own Anthony Perkins, was originally cast as Bobby, while Dean Jones, who was going through a divorce at the time he opened the Broadway run, was quickly replaced with gay actor Larry Kert, who then took the production to the West End). That out gay actors like Esparza, in Doyle's revival; John Barrowman, in a well-received Kennedy Center run; and Neil Patrick Harris, in a New York Philharmonic concert performance that was broadcast again on PBS, have also taken a stab at Bobby—and gained plaudits for their soulful renditions—has long added to the sense that the quandary *Company* posits rests on a queer(ed) center.

Seeing Bobby as a gay man—a closeted one, even—could, theoretically, "solve" the problem at hand. "You Could Drive a Person Crazy," a song that lists all the reasons why Bobby's girlfriends could excuse his reticence toward settling down (with any one of them), spells it out explicitly: they could understand a person not wanting to be tied down if that person was, as per the original lyrics, "a fag." Even the more up-to-date version of that line (which changes it to noting that they'd understand it if a person *happened* to be gay) maintains the same spirit of the complaint.

Time Out critic Adam Feldman, commenting on Harris's casting ahead of the 2013 concert, traced this very queered casting history, suggesting that "Bobby's straightness seems a requirement of the plot but not of the character"—a result no doubt of the personal experience both Furth and Sondheim brought to the straitlaced material—concluding that "in some ineffable way, that is why gay men posing as straight on stage have connected with it most effectively." One wonders what would've happened had the all-male (read: gay) version of the show Roundabout Theatre workshopped in 2014 been fleshed out into a full-blown production. As it stands, the only queered vision of *Company* audiences have been able to entertain is in the recent Marianne Elliot production, which flipped Bobby into Bobbie and Amy into Jamie, giving actors Jonathan Bailey (on the West End) and Matt Doyle (on Broadway) the chance to turn "Getting Married Today" into a post–*Obergefell v. Hodges* gay-riddled cocktail of anxiety over the now more pressing need to assimilate and conform. "Just because we can doesn't mean we should," Jamie tells Paul in Elliot's revival. Of course, even though they know they don't need to, they still go ahead and tie the knot.

Maybe this is why I so gravitate still to Esparza's portrayal of Bobby, who is both eager and hesitant about leaving his cozy if lonely spot on the sidelines. The cool detachment Bobby so calls for was not so much mellowed by his performance as archly ironized. You can see how Esparza connected viscerally with Bobby. In a *New York Times* profile, the actor spoke candidly about how he'd spent the better part of his adult life trying to come to terms with his sexuality (he'd had male lovers before) while needing to maintain a specific facade for his family (he'd married his high school sweetheart). Speaking of the truth he found in the lyrics of "Marry Me a Little," Esparza waxed poetic about the bittersweet proposal there concealed: "It seems so practical," he told the *Times*. "It gets me right in the gut. I know what that's like, to be in a relationship and know there is something seriously wrong here, but I don't want to acknowledge it, because if I do I'll have to talk about it. Let's not talk about it, and it'll be all right. And you know what? It can be all right for a long time and not just all right, great. And then one day, you're not." For Esparza, and for Bobby, perhaps, marriage is most alluring when it's a pragmatic proposal, when it's bracketed from romance and lust, from love and desire. That's how it can best be made to last. Hidden within the lyrics of "Marry Me a Little" is, in fact, quite a modern vision of marriage. Bobby pleads with Amy to marry him, as the title of the song suggests, just a little. Just enough, in fact. There'll be crying, but hopefully not too often. And there'll be play, but it won't be too rough. He even suggests they keep a tender distance, the better for the both of them to remain free. In his mind, that's the way it ought to be. Ideally, they won't have to give up a thing and they'll be able to stay who they are. There's a wistful desperation in Esparza's voice, in Bobby's words, in Sondheim's song. This bachelor is reaching for the most elastic version of a marriage, of a partnership, of what company can look like between two people. But maybe that's why it ultimately falls on deaf ears. He's still stuck in thinking in twos.

For in that gap is the kernel of possibility *Company* revolves around. Triangulation is the structure of the show: not just those three girlfriends we meet and who sing and dance (or play instruments) together but the many threes Bobby is constantly called to round out. It is through those thirds that the well-worn intimacies of a partnership can be strengthened. In his study on monogamy, Adam Phillips argues that "coupledom is a performance art," a fitting aphorism that sounds right even as it feels rather vacuous; we become keen observers when called to be someone else's "better half." But as weddings constantly remind us, you also have to be two to others, not just to yourselves. A couple as such then requires an audience. Which is precisely what Bobby is called to be—and called out for being. Why not pursue that further, to its limit case? Why not take up the idea Bobby flirts with in "Marry Me a Little" to create a marriage that's rooted in closeness *and* distance, and that allows space not only for you to be who you are and wish to be but to pursue desires outside of the couple? One is impossible and two is dreary, Bobby sings in "Side by Side by Side"—an ode to the complicated arithmetic of marriage. It's three, then, that's safe and cheery. Three, in fact, *is*—or can be!—company.

8.

THREE'S A CROWD

THE DAY I TOLD MY HUSBAND I HAD CHEATED WAS THE DAY I knew my marriage was over. With my confession (much too belated, much too belabored) I derailed the happily-ever-after that was supposed to have followed our wedding close to five years prior. Years of therapy have encouraged me to reframe such a statement, though: there's a way to tell this story so that the marriage was over before my utterance, before I even stepped out and outright became an adulterer. Another where the admission was the beginning of the end only because there wasn't enough understanding on the part of my partner. Another still where such demarcations are futile and useless; better to dissect the journey rather than its heartbreaking milestones, no?

There are infinite variations wherein that fateful day doesn't mark an ending. But I still feel confident and contrite enough to shoulder the blame for my marriage's demise. It was I who strayed. It was I who lied. It was I who betrayed. The details are not for me to divulge or spend ink here unspooling. For the general arc of what I went through is unspeakably familiar. Stories about infidelity rooted in one partner's restlessness and their frustrated desires are a dime a dozen. They're so common they're clichéd. Which makes having lived through such a tale not only painful but dispiriting. Didn't I know better? Didn't I know how this would end? Didn't I know *that* this would end?

When I confessed to my indiscretions (just as obliquely as I have in these pages, details feeling as unnecessary here and now as they did then and there), my partner and I were faced with the question of what to do, with how to narrativize what had happened. *Had I cheated?* for instance, or *Was I a cheater?* Was the issue *that* I had cheated or *why* I had done so? These didn't feel like pedantically semantic questions to me as they did to him. They keyed into how to understand what I'd done (who I'd been) and what would have to be done (who I'd have to become) in order to move forward. The reason I knew my marriage would be over the moment I confessed was obvious to me: I had crossed the one line a committed partner is not supposed to cross. Monogamy—and I'd willingly agreed to such an arrangement—remains the pillar of how we value and are meant to secure our erotic and romantic intimacies. We demand fidelity of one another not so much as proof of our love but as proof of our commitment to such love.

Adam Phillips, who wrote an entire book called *Monogamy*, understands the hold such a concept has on our everyday lives. For him, to examine what it means to be committed to just one other person is a way to look outward into how we organize our world: "Monogamy is a kind of moral nexus," he writes, "a keyhole through which we can spy on our preoccupations." It is an inquiry into the word *we*, which occasionally comes to the fore at the expense of our singular *I*. More aphoristic than it has any right to be, Phillips's tome is a collection of thought snippets meant to be teased out by the reader. Some are best left alone ("A couple is a conspiracy in search of a crime. Sex is often the closest they can get") while others demand to be turned over and thought through to their logical conclusion. Take his assertion that "infidelity is such a problem because we take monogamy for granted." The issue, he writes, is that "we treat it as the norm." But there might be a better way: "Perhaps we should take infidelity for granted, assume it with unharassed ease. Then we would be able to think about monogamy." (It is telling, he notes, that we think of monogamy as the opposite of infidelity, and not, more productively, the opposite of bigamy or polygamy.) This is no doubt easier to do in the abstract, divorced from the emotional thorns that plague us when we're faced with the fallout following infidelity in practice. Nowadays—and now more literally divorced from those conversations—I have been interested in how monogamy architects a rather restrictive vision of intimacy between a couple. In fact, it constructs intimacy between two that weds commitment and sexual exclusivity, often without much thought given to what that means. And so, anything that falls outside becomes an attack on the very foundations on which a twosome is built.

In a probing, provocative article about adultery from the late 1990s—when sex scandals had once more made such private concerns into wildly public affairs—cultural critic Laura Kipnis raged against the codified confines of modern marriages. She took aim at the notion that (good) marriages "take work." Rather than a helpful imperative, Kipnis saw a rhetorical twist that made us all into willing emotional laborers: "If you're working at monogamy," she writes, "you've already entered a system of exchange: an economy of intimacy governed—as such economies are—by scarcity, threat, and internalized prohibitions; secured ideologically—as such economies are—by incessant assurances that there are no viable alternatives. When monogamy becomes work, when desire is organized contractually, with accounts kept and fidelity extracted like labor from employees, with marriage a domestic factory policed by means of rigid shop-floor discipline designed to keep the wives and husbands of the world choke-chained to the reproduction machinery—this is a somewhat different state of affairs than Happy Marriage."

Kipnis's language, not to mention her imagery, is a bit too brutal (though how evocative is it to figure marriage as a "domestic factory"?). But she keenly keys into the logical conclusion of how we understand marriage in the late twentieth and early twenty-first century: as a contract. While writing this book, I've attended three weddings in three different countries. Each was boldly modern, eschewing many social, cultural, and religious traditions. But in so doing, in making them more personal, the couples laid bare the very labor Kipnis diagnoses. Detailed and touching vows about how their partners were their everything—their best friends, their confidants, their cheerleaders, not to mention would-be co-parents, travel companions, and an exhaustive list of many other job requirements—were nakedly earnest yet not, for that, any less exacting. Those are a lot of roles to fulfill, not to mention to be asked to fulfill well. Every day. For the rest of one's life.

What's curious to observe, though, is how little airtime monogamy and sexual exclusivity get in these weddings. Even, or especially, when it is so obviously called to anchor such a match. Many of us may not immediately think of monogamy as labor, as Kipnis suggests, but there's no denying that many of us understand how hard it can be, and harder still to sustain. There is, perhaps, no greater advocate for such a stance than Dan Savage, the sex columnist whose views on commitment, marriage, and coupledom have incited as much ire as inspiration for the past few decades. "Monogamy is harder than we admit," Savage posited in the pages of *The New York Times*. It's why he'd been "articulating a sexual ethic that he thinks honors the reality, rather than the romantic ideal, of marriage." Savage, who's often boasted about the "monogamish" relationship he and his husband, Terry, have jointly built with each other over time, has long been an advocate for examining why sexual exclusivity remains such a stalwart pillar of how and why we value coupledom—rather than succumbing to our knee-jerk condemnations of infidelity. Over the years, through his column, "Savage Love," readers have come to learn that the Seattle-based writer is wholly committed to commitment (he wrote a book so titled in 2005!) but also understands that there's a need for pliability when extolling the virtues of finding someone you're eager to spend your life with. For starters, he's prone to dispensing with the idea that we're all looking for "the one": "There is no perfect person out there for you, no ideal partner, no soul mate waiting to be found, no one person capable of meeting all of your emotional, sexual, and social needs," he writes in his book *Savage Love from A to Z*. It's the rigidity of how we're blindly encouraged to think of our relationships, Savage advises time and time again, that often places readers in the dire emotional situation that drives them to write in to his advice column. It's not that Savage is intent on breaking down the myth of monogamy. It's that he wants us all to be more wary of seeing any small cracks in its veneer as proof that something would obviously need to change. But he acknowledges how hard that can be, especially since to go against monogamy—to cheat, really—is so easily understood as a selfish and therefore inexcusable choice.

More obvious than being stories about people being selfish, though, stories about infidelity are stories about the self. Or so popular culture likes to tell us. If marriage plots thrust us toward endings wherein two become one, those about adultery frame themselves as moments when that two fractures back into one. Or, better yet, as tales wherein a twosome feels all too claustrophobic, pushing one (or the other) into a story where they can be not just singular but maybe even single once more. On the page—not to mention on the

stage and on-screen—infidelity becomes a mobilizing force to rekindle one's own identity; it becomes an excuse to refashion oneself in
one's image, not a familiar other's—one that borrows as much from a
remembered past as from an imagined or desired future. Away from
the stifling familiarity a committed relationship can proffer, infidelity
opens up new possibilities, new stories. It may also shed light on the
way one's own story, one's own relationship, may be in dire need
of a rewrite. Perhaps that's why we have a hard time folding those
moments back into our lives—because we'd rather keep them *as* moments rather than beginnings (which would force you to start from
scratch) or endings (which, as I can attest, may well force you to do
the same). But here I go again being swept away by Sondheimian
language, echoing the way in which one of his most famed adulteresses self-examines her own choices when faced with a moment in
the woods with a man who's not her husband, who's not her baker.

Into the Woods, Stephen Sondheim and James Lapine's land-
mark 1987 musical centered on witches and giants and princes and
many other fairy-tale characters, is very much about the constricting nature of well-worn stories, about how happily ever afters tell
only half the tale. How getting one's wish may be as much a bless-
ing as a curse. If act 1 finds many of its characters willfully pursuing the wishes they hope to make come true, act 2 scrambles their
many plots to reveal how such wishes (such endings) may need to be
amended. Take the Baker and his wife. At the start of the musical, all
they wish for is a child (for their family tree, as we're told, to not be a
barren one); yet by the time the curtain's back up after intermission
and the two travel back to the middle of the woods, fearful of a giant
in their midst, the Baker's Wife ends up in the arms of Cinderella's
Prince, a cad of a man who has eyes for any pretty maiden who
comes his way. Ensnared by the charming ways of that charming
prince, she cannot fathom the situation—the moment!—she's in. She

sings as much, voicing her concerns to this wily prince and to the audience alike, pointing out how ridiculous the entire scene feels. What could she possibly be doing there? Kissing the prince makes her feel like she's ventured not just far from her life but far from her own narrative. The funny aside that follows—about how she's in the wrong story!—was cribbed from an observation by actress Joanna Gleason, the original Baker's Wife. And, in its comedy, it gets at the way Sondheim and Lapine's central couple are clearly out of sorts and out of place. The Baker and his wife are wholly contemporary (neurotic, even!) figures thrust into stories that are, as the Baker's Wife tells Cinderella's Prince, all too wrong for them, for her. She's supposed to be a dutiful wife (note her character name) and a loving, doting mother (hence her wish). There are vows and ties and needs and standards, she insists, as much to herself as to her rapt audience. There are even plenty of *shouldn'ts* and *shoulds*. She's not supposed to be throwing caution to the wind and kissing a stranger in the middle of the woods, no matter how handsome he may be. She'd arrived, after all, at the end she had desperately wanted to inhabit at the start of the musical. Why risk it?

But her moment in the woods with the prince alights something within the Baker's Wife. She's been pining and curious about him since she'd first happened upon Cinderella, after all. While being seduced by him, she gets a taste of what another life would (could!) be. But that, in a nutshell, is what affairs afford us, and what Esther Perel, in her wide-ranging book on the subject, *The State of Affairs: Rethinking Infidelity*, suggests. "When we select a partner, we commit to a story," she writes. "Yet we remain forever curious: What other stories could we have been part of? Affairs offer us a window into those other lives, a peek at the stranger within." Sondheim and Lapine's protagonist understands as much. Could that really have been him? Have been her? Could a prince really have kissed her? Was it wrong? Is she mad? These are all rhetorical questions she ponders once he leaves her to question what exactly took place. Surely, they're all meant to be answered in the affirmative. She knows this and yet she needs to work it out, in song, of course, which is how Sondheim's obscenely self-aware characters come to break down their actions, their feelings about their actions, and the many reactions they have to such critical reminiscences.

Where does adultery belong in a fairy tale? In the woods, according to Sondheim's lyrics. In the solo that follows her tryst with the prince, the Baker's Wife ponders what it means to have fallen prey to her own unruly desires. She may have been in the wrong story but maybe that is very much the point of living, the ability to constantly fall into (and, crucially, leap out of) moments in the woods where you learn who you are and what you want. But what she learns is that rigid ideals are hard to adhere to. Sondheim's playful lyrics take this further. Every time the Baker's Wife (whether in the wry, rueful ways of Gleason in the original production, the giddy energy of Amy Adams in the Shakespeare in the Park revival, or even the bright, sunny warmth of Emily Blunt's big-screen rendition) sings about where she finds herself living out this story, she stresses the fine homonymous line that exists between "woods" and "woulds."

Those "woulds" are in constant tension with the "shouldn'ts and shoulds" the Baker's Wife knows structure her own story. "Moments in the Woods" is a song about possibility. Why are our choices rooted in *or* rather than *and*? Why can't it be both? Why *can't* we have it all? Or reach for it, however imperfectly? Of course, the lesson the Baker's Wife learns by the end of the song is about embracing those possibilities and then making presumably safer, more responsible choices accordingly: she's to go back to life, back to sense, back to child, back to husband, away from those woods.

The show doesn't allow her to follow through with this realization, though. For shortly after she sings this verse, as she wanders back toward the life she's had and now desperately wants again, she's felled by the Giant wreaking havoc all over those woods. Is there some moralizing in her death? Had she escaped temptation (either earlier or altogether), she might have survived. She might have come out of the woulds unscathed.

Show and character alike want us to dismiss the prince's seemingly careless ways. To live a life of just moments (every now and then a bad one) is unsustainable, the musical posits. Life can't be made of only moments, the Baker's Wife tells us in "Moments in the Woods." For if that were the case, you would never be able to tell them apart; they wouldn't—couldn't!—stand out. Life needs ebbs and flows. Or rather, a kind of steady baseline for any kind of moment (in the woods or elsewhere) to really feel like it matters, like it's offering you something truly novel. The world of *ands* is presented as transient. As only possible within the spatial and narrative limits of the woods. The musical, focused as it is on family structures (on the centrality of children, no less!), pushes its characters toward domesticity. In fact, a rather cynical reading of "Moments in the Woods" would find us seeing the Baker's Wife as finally domesticating her desires in the service of her Baker, of her child, of her home. The thrilling possibility she allows herself to imagine when she argues she could have a baker for bread and a prince for whatever (usually played for laughs, the role calling for canny comedic actresses who can lightly make such self-deprecating humor sing) evaporates almost immediately as a somewhat silly proposition, as one best dispensed with.

In Sondheim and Lapine's world, the woods are full of woulds. They are the place characters go to get their wishes. They are the place where anything can and does happen: A space where a young maiden can become a princess. Where a young lad can line his pockets with gold. Where a witch can get her beauty back. But as the Baker's Wife sings, you can't stay in the woods. You can't live in the woulds. You need to commit. You eventually have to get back to your story, to your Baker, to your child. Romance, as the Baker's Wife finds out, remains the only kind of story that would push her away from her mundane family life. In this, Sondheim and Lapine's character is merely playing out a centuries-old tale. Not one rooted in childish fairy tales but in grown-up novels that concern themselves with mapping out the budding modern marriage plot. She may well be a twentieth-century response to the likes of Anna Karenina and Madame Bovary, fated women whose affairs befell them.

It's in those classic novels that Western literature most acutely presented how women's lives were circumscribed by the very confines of marriage, as contract and bondage. For literary critic Tony Tanner, there is no way of understanding the novel as we know it without discussing how concerned it was with marriage—and with adultery. Marriage, he writes, "is a means by which society attempts to bring into harmonious alignment patterns of passion and patterns of property; in bourgeois society it is not only a matter of putting your Gods where your treasure is . . . but also of putting your libido, loyalty, and all other possessions and products, including children, there as well. For bourgeois society marriage is the all-subsuming, all-organizing, all-containing contract. It is the structure that maintains the Structure." Marriage, for Tanner, is the narrative structure of bourgeois society and, therefore, the organizing principle of its most novel storytelling genre: the novel! Here you could think of everything from early epistolary novels, like Samuel Richardson's *Pamela; or, Virtue Rewarded* and Pierre Choderlos de Laclos's *Les Liaisons dangereuses,* or later more canonical entries by the likes of

George Eliot, Jane Austen, and the Brontë sisters, to notice how central the question of marriage—its imperative as a principle in bourgeois life—was to the very creation of the novel.

But even in scouring such scant examples (and we could name more), you can't escape the way this narrative form often reveals itself as obsessed with the gaps within this idea of marriage as a narrative and societal structure, depicting and interrogating the transgressions it engenders and allows. Having focused on protagonists who struggled against the confines of the society they inhabit (often being pushed into marriage as an aspirational model for an ending, happy or otherwise), the novel, in Tanner's eyes "moves toward marriage and the securing of genealogical continuity" even as it "often gains its particular narrative urgency from an energy that threatens to contravene that stability." This is why it is but a paradoxical object in society, "by no means an inert adjunct to the family décor, but a text that may work to subvert what it seems to celebrate." Marriage was central to the birth—and to the evolution—of the novel. But only through stories that hinged on its transgressions, on its failures, on its failed promises, perhaps. There is no marriage (nor novel) without adultery. For the novel as a form thrived on these visions of narrative possibility, of futurities imagined and pursued. What better figure to exemplify that but the adulteress. Not the mistress, mind you. Not the lover nor the whore. Those are all character tropes well known and well accounted for. No, the adulteress becomes the novelistic figure par excellence in the bourgeois novel precisely because she's an impossibility. Because she's reduced to an action and not an identity. An action, in fact, that puts her at odds with what she's supposed to be and stand for: a loving wife, a doting mother.

It's telling that at the start of the twenty-first century, Tom Perrotta, in writing a novel about a woman, dissatisfied with her own marriage, who carelessly throws herself into an affair with the stay-at-home dad all the women in her neighborhood fawn and gossip over, turns to what Tanner dubs as "the most important and far-reaching novel of adultery in Western literature": Gustave Flaubert's seminal 1857 novel, *Madame Bovary*. *Little Children*'s Sarah (played in the film adaptation by Kate Winslet, an actress whose on-screen work could very much be described as capturing the many vexing vices of wayward desires) is adrift in her own life. She's unsure how she came to be a housewife who spends her days with her young daughter wistfully daydreaming of what could have been. Spurred, in part, by the realization her husband has a pornography addiction, she falls headfirst into an affair with the "Prom King," the handsome dad at the playground who's struggling with his own sense of self at home (his dreams of passing the bar and becoming a lawyer seem to be receding, if they were ever there at all). As Sarah, a former graduate student, finds her lust for life rekindled by her affair, she's invited to a neighborhood book club where she's forced to reassess Flaubert's novel, which she'd not much cared for at school. Revisiting it in light of her own recent choices—and driven to scold the way the women in her book club so dismiss Flaubert's protagonist as a "slut"—Sarah makes an impassioned plea to see her instead as a feminist icon.

"Oh, that's nice. So now cheating on your husband makes you a feminist?" one of the women in the club says, perhaps seeing right through Sarah's self-mythologizing. But it allows Perrotta to give voice to how his protagonist is reframing Flaubert's Emma in her own mind: "No. It's not the cheating," she insists. "It's the *hunger. The hunger for an alternative.* And the refusal to accept a life of unhappiness." In Perrotta's prose, there is no way of uncoupling Sarah's feelings about Emma Bovary without hearing her own explanation for why she's let herself be so entangled with that handsome Prince Charming, er, Prom King. In Todd Field's film adaptation, the book club discussion segues into one of the film's many omniscient voice-over narrations: "Sarah sometimes let herself be carried away by fantasies of a future very different from the life she was living now. A future without obstacles, in which she and Brad were free to love each other in broad daylight. In which all the mistakes of the past were erased, and they had no one to answer to but each other." Here is the alternative she allows herself to imagine, the one she's currently hungering for. It doesn't matter that it's a fanciful fantasy. That's the allure of an affair. It's why for Perel, adultery is "the revenge of the deserted possibilities." (Oh but why must they remain deserted? Why might we not find ways of recovering them?)

Therein lies the anxiety that curdles in both Emma and in Sarah. These two characters, separated by close to 150 years, are kindred spirits because they look back on the women they were with anguish. But also with hunger. Flaubert's title is a provocation in itself; Emma finds her marital moniker to be an ill-fitting garment, one she wishes she could discard and so return her to being that beautiful girl who oh so many men admired. Emma, as Joyce Carol Oates has described her, is "a finely drawn portrait of a woman doomed to unhappiness in love. Emma is corrupted not by any actual man but by her reading; she yearns to locate, in the world, the elusive image of romantic passion." Emma, like Sarah, yearns for what's so far gone. Or, as Tanner figures it, there comes a moment when it can be said that "what is far will appeal to Emma more than what is near, that memory reconstitutes itself as desire, that in an impossible way she will be trying to displace herself from presence to distance, to bring herself near to the 'far.'"

Such a line rings especially true for me. Closeness, which is what we're always meant to aspire to, can feel restricting. Intimacy boxes us in. Or can, if we so let it. If we don't cultivate it right. As Perel points out, "Affairs are an act of betrayal and they are also an expression of longing and loss." To those women in Sarah's book club—and maybe to many readers of this book—that latter clause may feel like an excuse for inexcusable behavior. But that yearning and that mourning Perel witnesses in her practice (she's a relationship therapist whose book is driven by real-life experiences derived from her many clients) is precisely what we tend to dismiss in these tales. Betrayal is easier to apprehend. Less so the idea that why you transgressed may be more crucial than the fact that you did.

For decades now, I've been obsessed with contemporary films about adulteresses. In contrast to clichéd stories about philandering men whose midlife crises result in laughably absurd affairs (*Fatal Attraction* being the most obvious example), films that center on lovelorn women who stray have long struck me as capturing—to borrow Sarah's musings on *Madame Bovary*—a decidedly radical way of thinking not only through the limits and limitations of traditional marriage but of those hungry feelings many of us quiet down within us until we can't anymore. Like *Little Children*, films like *Concussion* (2013), *Notes on a Scandal* (2006), and *Unfaithful* (2002) are interested in what their characters, and their audience, can learn *from* affairs. Sadly the lesson tends to be the same almost every single time. Awash in lives that feel arrested, these women find enticements outside the home, ones that make them feel like never before, like strangers in their own skin. In Stacie Passon's 2013 film, a concussion is what first drives well-adjusted and happily married Abby (Robin Weigert) to not just have sex with women who are not her wife but to charge for such exchanges. Those kinds of freedoms, lurid and furtive as they may be, rekindle something in these women—they become strangers to themselves in ways that feel nourishing. "I've been good all my adult life. I've been a decent wife, dutiful mother," *Notes on a Scandal*'s Sheba (Cate Blanchett) tells her friend Barbara (Judi Dench) when recounting the start of her affair with a fifteen-year-old student. "Why shouldn't you be bad? Why shouldn't you transgress? You've earned the right," she comforts herself. But what's at first a thrill—the kind that gives *Unfaithful*'s Connie (Diane Lane) blush-worthy feelings that commingle ecstatic satisfaction with guilt-riddled embarrassment as she takes the train back to her loving husband following her first tryst in the city with an unspeakably dashing young man—soon becomes not an answer to a question about who they wanted to be and who they wanted to want, but a problem best solved so as to maintain what they already have and who they've already got.

These protagonists are no longer doomed to the tragic fates of Emma Bovary or Anna Karenina (even of the Baker's Wife!). But their endings are no less bleak. In oh so many of these stories, affairs are wayward detours from these characters' everyday lives that crystallize what these women *truly* want, *truly* need, *truly* can't live without. Namely: their partners, their children, their home. To borrow the Baker's Wife's language, they've all been able to have an *and* and are now back to *or*, which ends up meaning so much more to them than it did before. The images Todd Field leaves us with in *Little Children*—Sarah hugging her daughter tight in bed before panning out of their suburban home to an empty playground at night—are tied to a final line that speaks to these very concerns. "You couldn't change the past," the film's omniscient narrator tells us. "But the future could be a different story. And it had to start somewhere."

If you watch enough of these films, you start to feel like there's only one way they may end, with the primacy of the nuclear family left intact, with resentment and embarrassment tidily drafting these women into the roles they had so briefly escaped. This is why I gravitate to Sarah Polley's *Take This Waltz*, a variation on this genre that refuses such a neatly structured ending. Like many of these other stories, Polley's 2011 Toronto-set film centers on a restless young woman, Margot (Michelle Williams), who struggles with keeping her increasingly intoxicating attraction to her studly neighbor in check. It doesn't help that her marriage to Lou (Seth Rogen) has settled into a version of domestic contentment that's as soothing as it is suffocating. Their bumbling sex life ("well choreographed" and "familiar" are the words Polley uses to describe their lovemaking in her screenplay) is made up of fits and starts, the two never quite finding the rhythms that had first brought them together, at times colliding with shared babyish language that both nurtures and neuters the intimacy they've built together. The two are stuck in a rote routine that Margot's chance meeting with Daniel (Luke Kirby) unsettles.

Polley's screenplay has a wonderful circularity to it. As written, she begins and ends with the same scene: Margot making blueberry muffins in her sweltering kitchen as a male figure hovers in the background. "The muffins rise," the screenplay reads. "She watches them, the expression on her face a curious mixture of peace, yearning, contentment, and longing." When we first watch the scene in the opening moments of the film, we're led to believe that this is Margot's life now, with Lou, a blend of comfort and dissatisfaction best encapsulated by the passing thrill of a home-baked good. But Polley circles back to this scene at the end of her script, using the same words to describe Margot's expression as she watches the muffins rise. Turns out the male figure in the shot wasn't Lou; it was Daniel. We've gone on a journey with Margot from one to the other and yet we find her in the same place we first met her. "New things get old," as her friend Geraldine (Sarah Silverman) had told her, "just like the old things did." As written, the script's recursiveness would suggest a structural restlessness that's inherent in Margot's life. But also, perhaps, in every- and anyone's relationship. Whatever she thought she'd accomplish by jumping into a life with Daniel (which, as one montage has shown us, was already wildly more sexually adventurous than her life with Lou) has eroded into the same kind of familiar domesticity she'd found so stifling to begin with.

In the finished film, though, Polley forgoes that circularity. Instead she follows the revisited muffins scene with a return to the Scrambler in Centre Island Margot had visited with Daniel. Margot (alone this time) is aboard the amusement ride while listening to the song that serves as the film's theme: "Video Killed the Radio Star." What's old has been replaced. The static shot forces us to focus on Margot's face, which goes from bemusement to wild abandon, with a final twinge of wistful melancholy. She's going round and round (like Polley's script first intended) but she's also standing (well, sitting) still. She's moving but in place. She's on a ride but isn't going anywhere. There's a thrill but it's controlled and contained. The metaphors and attendant questions Polley calls up in this final shot are plentiful. Is Margot doomed to be in this relationship merry-go-round forever? Is passion something that inherently wanes, waxes, and then disappears altogether? Is she truly a "lunatic," as Geraldine tells her, for wanting to fill the gap she senses in her life, which her friend submits is but a fact? "Life has a gap in it. It just does. You don't go crazy trying to fill it!" she'd been warned.

There's no way of thinking or talking about *Take This Waltz* without thinking and talking about Polley's follow-up project, the autobiographical documentary about her mother (and her mother's long-known, open-secret extramarital affair that had resulted in Polley's own birth). *Stories We Tell* was released a year after *Take This Waltz*. The two works have always existed, in my mind at least, as twinned interrogations on adultery. The two projects, after all, concern themselves with the elasticity of marital fidelity and with the lengths (some) women will go to rekindle in themselves a spark their partners may be dimming if not outright extinguishing. Knowing Polley learned about her mother's affair—and that the dad she'd always known wasn't her biological father—while creating a documentary project about the mom she only knew in childhood (Diane Polley died the week the actress-turned-filmmaker turned eleven) cannot help but color the emotional framework for *Take This Waltz*. What's most enthralling about these two tales is the tender earnestness with which Polley tells them. There's no rancor or shame in the way Margot's and Diane's respective affairs are presented. Polley lends an empathetic ear to their stories: she understands viscerally how brave these women would have to be to look at their lives and wish for more and, however imperfectly, reach for it. In *Stories We Tell*, one of Polley's sisters tears up talking about how she enjoys knowing her mother had found the love she was aching for in her own marriage, an admission that doesn't neglect the emotional wreckage she left behind but acknowledges the truth of the matter without the recrimination that would usually follow such a statement—a statement that would make, I think, Dan Savage proud.

This is Polley's strength as a storyteller, something her directorial debut, 2006's *Away from Her* had already proven. The film was adapted from Alice Munro's "The Bear Came Over the Mountain," from the 2001 short story collection *Hateship, Friendship, Courtship, Loveship, Marriage*. Story and film center on an aging couple, Fiona and Grant (Julie Christie and Gordon Pinsent). The two have lived a full life together for five decades. Now, with Fiona's Alzheimer's getting worse, the two decide to relocate her to a home where, for her first thirty days there, she will have to do without Grant's visits. By the time Grant returns, she's all but forgotten him and has formed a strong bond with another man living there. Grant is at first baffled and rightly irritated—at her, at himself, at their circumstances. But he soon grows to accept the cold indifference she greets him with, only at times wondering whether it's a ruse, a way to get back at him for all those affairs he'd had years ago. When Fiona's other man gets transferred out by his wife, Grant has to grapple with how to help a now depressed and depleted Fiona—even as he later comes to form a close bond, as well, with Fiona's erstwhile lover. Polley fleshes out this latter part of Fiona and Grant's story, which Munro had only touched on in her piercingly honest short story. The couple at the heart of the story—which Polley has said is "the most interesting and complex portrait of a marriage" she'd ever read—have and continue to make allowances for each other. Grant, in Munro's words, is a philanderer who nevertheless launders his past indiscretions in language that belies his lack of agency ("An epidemic had broken out," is how he writes about men stepping out on their marriage, "it was spreading like the Spanish flu"). And it's shortly thereafter that Munro suggests, if ever so briefly, that Fiona may have been aware of what was happening ("Fiona was quite willing," she writes. "And Grant himself did not go overboard").

Polley further complicates that diplomatic emotional détente in her film by having Grant get involved with Fiona's lover's wife, opening up possibilities about how marriage can work on different terms, just as she would later do in *Take This Waltz* and *Stories We Tell*. Here is an openness fueled by circumstance, an affront to monogamy that feels rooted in compassion rather than indignation. Here is a portrait of love that endures precisely because it doesn't foreclose visions of *and*s. Polley's filmography has always appealed to me because her narratives fold in on themselves. She's always writing about writing, telling stories about the way we tell stories—which is how I best apprehend core emotional truths, by the way they're narrativized (in one's mind, on a screen, on the page). It's no surprise to find that her Oscar-winning screenplay for *Women Talking* rests on this artistic tenet: "Your story will be different than ours" is the line that closes that film about the brave choice a group of Mennonite women make in the face of unspeakable horrors. And in *Run Towards the Danger: Confrontations with a Body of Memory*, her memoir-in-essays, she asks, in earnest, "Why do we write things about ourselves? To absolve ourselves of guilt? To confess? To right a wrong? To be heard? To apologize? To clarify things for ourselves or others?"

I've been wrestling with those questions myself. Particularly in a chapter where I come out as an adulterer—even if I don't share specific details about what kind of nudes I sent and to whom; whose flirtations I allowed to go past the line of propriety and when (or how many times); what hotel room I ended up at that one time; and what kind of self-prescribed limits I imposed on myself while visiting bathhouses in different countries. This project was born from the desire to make sense of my desires. I was never so much searching for romantic passion, as Oates suggests Flaubert's protagonist is, for I was not looking for romance. But I was looking for passion even if such yearning (frustrating as it was, framed as futile as it always is) was supposedly ephemeral and thus not worth pursuing. Our language for it betrays us: passion burns hot and thus eventually fizzles. Or it's fiery and can therefore scald you. It's painful and demands sacrifices of you, especially if you're in a committed monogamous relationship, as I was. But to even tell my story I need to resort to language that leaves me unable to escape its biases. If I say I strayed, I conjure up a path I was supposed to stay on. If I write about indiscretions, I already admit I lacked better judgment. If I claim myself as an adulterer, I bring up notions of pollution, of soiling and befouling something meant to be kept pristine. If I used the word *cheater*, I vocalize how I opted to play outside the rules. It's always baffling (though utterly understandable) how stories about affairs so seldom push us to think outside of the rules of engagement an affair so clearly upends.

What if instead of reifying the labor of monogamy they imagined, instead, an approach driven by more leisure (and pleasure)?

At the end of Denis de Rougemont's titillating *Love in the Western World*, an examination of the myths about love and passion, about marriage and adultery that have been passed down (and perhaps been degraded and eroded in the process) through centuries of Western culture, the Swiss writer and critic ends on a remarkably sunny note. Aware that his polemic may strike some as dour and pessimistic about the state of romance at the time of its writing (1938, though he'd come to revise the monograph again in 1954 and 1972), de Rougemont reaches for a kind of positive horizon to look to: "A fidelity maintained in the Name of what does not change as we change will gradually disclose some of its mystery," he writes, "*beyond tragedy another happiness awaits.* A happiness resembling the old, but no longer belonging to the form of the world, for this new happiness transforms the world." In his mind, such a world transformed is one pulled by the Christian vision of love (agape) that stands in contrast with the fiery (and thus destructive) figure of eros, that passion that shackles us away from fidelity to one another. But we can be more imaginative—and more permissive and more expansive—than de Rougemont and the many thinkers and writers who so believe in such baseless dichotomies.

Could we stay in the woods? Could we find a way to explore those woulds we'd never have let ourselves daydream about in our relationships, in our homes, in our lives? Could we find ways to push back against the dichotomies that rule tired old tales about adultery (between, as Phillips notes in *Monogamy*, "safety and danger, habit and passion, love and lust, attachment and desire")? Could we not embrace them all if we didn't pit them against one another? Why are we to have one but not the other?

As the Baker's Wife sings, why not aim for both instead?

9.

THREE'S COMPANY

THROUPLE IS A WEIRD WORD.

The cheeky expression blends *three* and *couple,* making any definition of it glaringly obvious. But the word's clunkiness speaks to the concept's own unwieldy definition. A couple is a twosome but a throuple isn't quite a threesome. There's a simplicity in the union of two: you can only draw one straight line between them. To try to join, let alone group, three people in any one relationship is messy business—and that's without me needing to trot out high school geometry to make my case.

Throuple is a word my boyfriends and I quite abhor. While I understand the impetus to fall back on such a neat portmanteau, I can't shake the way it ends up conjuring (in my head at least) a kind of fuzzy nineties-style monster (think Furby) or a furry seventies piece of furniture (maybe I'm thinking of velour futons?). When I began dating a couple—a sentence I never foresaw myself uttering, let alone jotting down in print—all three of us agreed that while such a concept would make us easily legible to others, we should seek another word, a better expression for what we had, for what we were building together. The internet was not particularly helpful. *Three-some* (like its French kin *ménage à trois*) calls up sexual athleticism. *Triad* makes us sound like villains in an episode of *Charmed*, while *bonus blend* has the hallmark of a small-batch-roasted coffee shop offering. Only *threelationship*, in its utter ridiculousness, seemed to capture the tricky math that goes into dating two people at the same time. Two people who, in my case, had already been an item for five years before they implausibly (and quite contentiously, as I would come to learn months later) had decided to "bring a third" into their home, into their life, into their relationship.

I like to joke that part of what led me to date a couple was the universe getting semantically petty with me. When my marriage was all but over and divorce was but a signed formality on the horizon, I remember telling my therapist (and any friend who'd curiously ask if I'd be looking to date anytime soon) that I wasn't really looking to date anyone. Any. One. It explains why I was so blindsided by the very absurd possibility of dating two that I didn't immediately shut it down. Part of it had to do with the fact that I didn't really realize we were on our way to dating until it was, alas, too late.

The question of *how* we began dating is a favorite of folks who likely struggle with the very story a throuple evokes. When such a question does come up—as it did during a leisurely walk with my sister, where my innocent and quite accurate assertion that we'd met at a bar didn't seem to appease her ("Okay, sure. But like, how did you start *dating* them, I mean?")—I know there's no way of escaping the torrid implications our tale bears out. I'm reminded here of a line from John Rechy's *The Sexual Outlaw*: "What's so alienating about homosexual relationships is that they begin with the intimacy of sex instead of proceeding toward it." Rechy, who's cheekily quoting a psychiatrist friend of his in that cruising manifesto of a nonfiction novel, is not entirely wrong. Not really. For romantic stories about threes (and here mine is no different) seem to always begin with sex. Sure, the most obvious example is, as we've seen, the tale of the affair, but that's not so much a story of threes as of ones and twos. Then again, that's how mine began as well.

I met my boyfriends at my sluttiest. My marriage had spectacularly collapsed and I was committed to living in a world of *ands* rather than *ors*. I was ready to say yes to any- and everything that came my way. Which is why, on this sweltering day in Palm Springs, where I was visiting a friend to celebrate his birthday, I opted to wear a white see-through bodysuit and a pair of body-hugging whitewashed denim shorts. It was as scandalous an outfit as I'd ever worn out in public—even as it was decidedly demure for a crowd all too used to seeing men parading themselves around in little more than a jockstrap and a matching grin. It was, as we like to recall it, a kind of twinned meet-cute: I hit it off chatting with one stranger right away, found myself handsy with the other but a while later. But unlike what meet-cutes call up usually, I didn't project myself into a future with either (let alone with both)—except as far as their bedroom, which I only reached a day later when they invited me over for drinks at their place. For how was I to know that there was a chance for more than a fun, steamy night (or two, or three) with two wildly attractive men who seemed all too glad to have found a pliable guy all too eager to please?

In my defense, unlike the myriad of rom-coms and marriage plot novels that have given me endless variations with which to imagine what could follow a meet-cute with a cute boy, there are few, if any, places to look to when it comes to how threelationships begin, bloom, and maybe even wither into oblivion. That's because at their core, any romantic (and even sexual) configuration that goes beyond two is suspect; it requires dispensing with so many of the narratives we've been told and have lived through. It demands you constantly be aware of how the world encourages and values twos; it makes little room, if any at all, for anything that strays from said norm. In a world that urges you to find your better half, opting to keep looking when you've found one makes you childish, makes you selfish, makes you greedy.

Had I not found myself in an emotional freefall, eager and able to deconstruct any and all inherited narratives about love and sex, I would not have been at a place where I could've conceived of, let alone embraced, the possibilities of a throuple. Divorce forces you to begin again. Rather than embitter me toward the intractability of monogamous twos (though it did), my divorce had me wondering what could be done to explode such a cultural template. Dutifully, then, I picked up a book I'd been eyeing for years: *The Ethical Slut.* Originally published in 1997, *The Ethical Slut* was conceived as its original subtitle suggests, "A Guide to Infinite Sexual Possibilities." Recent editions have tweaked said subtitle but the tome remains an interrogation and introduction to its titular figure (an intentionally chosen oxymoron of a concept: Who'd imagine a slut to be ethical?). For decades now, Dossie Easton and Janet Hardy have been committed to talking openly about how we can all build intimacies (sexual and otherwise) with a theory of abundance in mind. As someone who'd found himself unable to curb his desires while shackled to the kind of relationship I'd told myself I had always aspired to, Easton and Hardy's insights felt novel and radical and refreshing. Emboldening, even. Moreover, in its very first chapter I saw the kind of language that would appeal to my own exploration of what could be found within the confines of ethical sluthood. "One of the most valuable things we learn from open sexual lifestyles," they write, "is that our programming about love, intimacy, and sex can be rewritten. When we begin to question all the ways we have been told we ought to be, we can begin to edit and rewrite our old tapes. By breaking the rules, we both free and empower ourselves."

My marriage plot had ended. But that didn't mean I couldn't start over. I needed only to think of how Torrey Peters dedicated her 2021 novel, *Detransition, Baby*, "to divorced cis women, who, like me, had to face starting their life over without either reinvesting in the illusions from the past, or growing bitter about the future." A few months after I had first devoured it upon release (my hardcover copy beams at me from my bookshelf as I type), I would return to that dedication and it would hit differently knowing I would soon become a divorced cis man—not exactly the person Peters had in mind, but I could nevertheless feel her words viscerally. The past was something I would soon have to leave behind (as I would the rented two-bedroom apartment we shared) and I'd have to embolden myself to reach for a vision of a possible future (alone in a rather modest one-bedroom pad). And to do so alone (lonely as well) without being able to afford wallowing in what that really meant. Beyond Peters's piercing insight on what matters of seismic self-fashioning can look like in adulthood aside, *Detransition, Baby* is a bold proposition of how we may begin to (re)imagine not just ourselves but the communities and families and intimate groupings we build around us.

At the center of the novel is an unlikely trio: Katrina, a newly divorced (and newly pregnant) woman whose partner Ames wishes to fold into their still budding relationship his motherhood-obsessed ex-girlfriend Reese, the trans woman who'd first helped him navigate New York City *as* a trans woman many years ago before he left her and detransitioned in quick succession. The novel's twinned narratives—neatly divided into descriptive time-bound titles ("Eight years before conception"; "Six weeks after conception," and so on)—are about how hard it can be to maintain and live in a couple, especially when each half of those various couples we read about are invested, in varying ways, in different modes of living in the world. For Peters, this was an inquiry into the preeminent American novelistic genre. As she explained to *Rolling Stone*, "A lot of the big American social novels are just these domestic novels, like Jonathan Franzen or whoever. They have these domestic themes which are usually around a bunch of assumptions about what it means to be American: nuclear families, middle class-ness, and all of these things that are sort of unexamined assumptions built into these books." She aimed to ask, "What happens when you put a trans woman into one of these domestic American social novels?" She knew that some things may be blown up but some others would remain the same.

To read *Detransition, Baby* while going through a divorce was particularly bruising. "When you get a divorce," Katrina tells Ames, "everyone expects you to provide a story to justify it." (And I had such a story: I'd cheated.) "But in real life," she continues, "the story and actual reasons for the divorce diverge. In reality everything is more ambivalent." Maybe I clung to the notion that my divorce was more ambivalent than I let myself believe because, as Peters so piercingly captured, sometimes such reasons and stories and ambivalences come from our inability to be honest with those who most wish us to be—and yet who'd be most hurt by such nakedly honest admissions. For in reading about how both Amy and Reese had, separately and almost in tandem, found ways to satiate their respective repressed desires away from each other (Amy with dommes she hired who gave her the erotic mothering she so needed, Reese with her brutish cis straight ex who made her feel taken and taken care of), I saw an all-too-familiar narrative. "She only felt a little guilt about wanting to see dommes," Peters writes of Amy, "because she believed that if she could simply achieve the needed release, she could return to Reese a whole girlfriend." The line rings true every time I revisit it; there's a crushing truth about how some of us had to (or felt we had to) navigate our illicit desires away from the comfort of our most intimate relationship. Two couldn't make room for more, but one needed more in order to make the two complete. This is how affairs bloom, with mental gymnastics and moral acrobatics making an Olympic athlete out of you. But what Amy and Reese hadn't realized—or couldn't let themselves face—was that there could possibly be a way to fold those urges into their own relationship. They could build a different kind of two that would allow them to find wholeness within and outside themselves without resorting to such betrayals, such lies, such affairs.

In writing about the thorny emotional triangle at the heart of Peters's torrid novel—a triangle that's pivoted not on the various sides Reese, Ames/Amy, and Katrina create with one another but on the child that brings them together—I stumbled onto yet another contemporary attempt to push us to think about a story of three. One similarly weighted and driven by a pregnancy. Ira Sachs has spent the better part of his career examining the grueling demands of long-term companionship. With films like *Married Life* (2007), *Keep the Lights On* (2012), and *Love Is Strange* (2014), Sachs has asked audiences to enter worlds where couples struggle with how to stay committed to one another when affairs, legal and romantic, sexual and financial, get in the way. With his most recent film, the Paris-set *Passages*, Sachs has repurposed many of his thematic motifs to offer a wounding story of an even bolder configuration: not one of (just) two but of three. The poster for the film bills it, according to one of the pull quotes plucked to better market it, as a "three-way tangle of desire and confusion." There's a couple here, yes (a gay male one, at that). But their entanglement with a flirty female stranger will soon upend their lives even as that encounter may finally bring them all together in ways they couldn't have anticipated.

When we first meet Tomas and Martin (Franz Rogowski and Ben Whishaw), they are stuck playing a well-rehearsed scene the two know all too well. At a wrap party for Tomas's film, Martin is spent. He has no interest in staying much longer at the bar where the cast and crew are celebrating. He has no energy with which to head to the dance floor with his husband, who's abuzz with adrenaline and excitement. And so, with few words exchanged, Martin leaves Tomas to enjoy the night on his own, as perhaps he's done many times before. When Tomas arrives home the next day, it's obvious Martin has suffered through this kind of interaction before. He's not so much upset at his partner as at himself for once again letting such immature exploits rankle him. Not that Tomas notices any of this. Self-involved almost to a fault, this wild and wily filmmaker is eager to share why he was out so late. Uninterested in keeping secrets or squirreling away the thrills of his late-night adventures, Tomas wants to include Martin in what appears to have been a life-changing outing: "You know what I was doing last night?" he asks Martin plainly. "I had sex with a woman. Can I tell you about it, please?" Rogowski hits that *please* with wide-eyed innocence. The question suggests the two have an open arrangement, though one guided, it seems, by a "don't ask, don't tell" policy. Only in this instance Tomas cannot abide by such rules. Given that Sachs has allowed us to witness Agathe (Adèle Exarchopoulos) and Tomas's bumbling and wholly steamy encounter the night before, we know why the moment has rattled the filmmaker who finds himself now smitten with a stranger yet lovingly committed still to his partner of many years.

"Can I tell you about it, please?" feels like a simultaneous opening and closing. On its surface, the question would seem to defuse emotional conflict. Tomas is all too candid. He wants to harbor no secrets. Not from Martin and not from himself. And not for any minute longer than necessary. But that's hard, especially for Martin. It's easy to hear a casual indifference in Tomas's query (Who would possibly want to hear about their partner's sexual exploits? Isn't he just rubbing it in?), but we should key into, instead, the world of radical honesty he's nudging Martin toward. In the last few months, I've been on both sides of that kind of discussion—on the one hand disclosing sexual escapades to my boyfriends with giddy excitement, on the other souring upon hearing of similar encounters that I was emotionally not well equipped to process at their same pace. To be open takes careful balance. What the question makes clear, though, is that Martin is most comfortable with not folding Tomas's extracurricular activities into their everyday lives. Especially not over breakfast as he's headed out the door. Those are narrative detours, subplots he'd rather not entertain as part of their shared life and story together.

It's why Martin is so wary of Tomas's insistence, let alone the cajoling way in which he frames his husband's expected response. "You could be happy for me," Tomas needles. Which seems like a callous kind of cruelty, proof of the self-involvement on display that makes no room for Martin's protestations. But that demand is also a way to bypass the clichéd conversations and fights this lisping, mesh-crop-top-wearing man-child of a director cannot abide by. Stories of threes that don't merely triangulate desire, or collapse into all-too-familiar tales of love and betrayal, are disorienting because they refuse the call toward known genres. Or a specific genre, at least. They rebuke, first and foremost, the siren song of melodrama. That's what Tomas represents. When Martin starts pouting and huffing, all Tomas asks of him is to not be melodramatic. There are other ways, such an imperative suggests, in dealing with the thorny feelings Tomas has and will soon further develop for this new woman in his life.

Later, when he gets Agathe pregnant and has to meet her parents, Tomas refuses to play the role of doting partner and supportive would-be father. He's prickly, unable to adhere to the bourgeois desires of Agathe's aghast parents. He can't promise he'll always be there for her, can he? He can't predict the future. All he can do is actually be there for her. Day in and day out. This is arguably what makes Tomas such a difficult character to understand, let alone sympathize with. It's why critics have called him everything from a "bad boyfriend" (*Vulture*) and a "flamboyant fuckboy" (*The Playlist*) to a "narcissist" (*The Guardian*) and a "borderline sociopath" (*Variety*). He's a character whose strident demeanor begs us to despise him. In this he's kin to *Detransition, Baby*'s Ames, someone who's so allergic to tropes and traditions that his imagined possibilities end up feeling like open admissions of how little patience he has for doing what's expected of him—even by and for those who love him.

Perhaps Richard Brody at *The New Yorker* best understood the possibilities unfurled by anchoring a film around Tomas: "With Tomas, Sachs has created a fictional character who's no alter ego but an ideal of sorts: he embodies the freedom of thought and action on which the very notion of art is based." For Brody, and I'm obviously inclined to agree, Tomas is friction incarnate; he's a catalyst unwilling to let things remain as they are. "Tomas turns out to be a sort of detonator of the emotional realm, who shatters the unchallenged core of settled lives and unleashes the energy that's stored up there." As played by Rogowski, this wayward film director is guileless. "This is a movie without shame," Sachs has explained, "in terms of both the images and the characters. Shame does not fuel this movie."

If his earlier films had been rooted in the illicit—with secrets and affairs eroding and corroding placid domesticity—*Passages* tries to imagine not just different configurations of desire but an entirely different playing field for such queries. Even in its triangulation, the image of a family Tomas dreams up is radical in its simplicity. In this he shares Ames's brazenness. And if they both are unsuccessful in the end, it is not for lack of trying. Theirs are images of a three that refuse neat and tidy conceptions of family and companionship—of parenthood, even. Which are, I must admit, in short supply.

Ever since I started dating two, I've been dutifully looking for more and different templates for what we could be building together. But polyamory—and the attendant consensual nonmonogamy we practice (we are quite a porous triangle, sexually at least)—remains on the margins of our shared pop culture imaginary. Throuples show up, most often, as punch lines (as in Billy Eichner's *Bros*) or as colorful side characters (as in Steven Rowley's *The Guncle*). They are curiosities, mostly. That is most definitely the case in musical theater's most obvious take on such an arrangement: *Cabaret*, which first debuted on Broadway back in 1966 has no doubt the most famous ode to throupledom the stage and screen has ever seen.

In that 1930s Berlin–set musical, based on Christopher Isherwood's pseudo-autobiographical novel *Goodbye to Berlin* (and its stage adaptation, John Van Druten's *I Am a Camera*), audiences get treated to "Two Ladies," an entire number devoted to what it means to live with two lovers. Meant as comedic commentary on the rooming arrangement wide-eyed singer Sally Bowles strikes up with bookish Cliff Bradshaw, "Two Ladies" finds the show's Emcee spelling out his own living situation with two of the dancers at the Kit Kat Club. Everyone in Berlin, he says, has a "perfectly marvelous roommate," borrowing the words Sally uses to ingratiate herself with the clueless American boy she handily seduces into letting her crash with him: Some people don't just have one person. Some have *two* people! The bubbly number finds humor in the juxtaposition of the domesticity its lyrics call up (focused as they are on who sleeps where and what chores everyone is in charge of) and the sexual innuendo the dance and orchestrations suggest. In the film adaptation, Joel Grey's Emcee spends much of the number under a giant sheet where we're to imagine what it is he and his "Two Ladies" do in their own shared bed; he even loses his pants midway through the number! In the 1993 Sam Mendes revival at the Donmar Warehouse in London (which later, with Rob Marshall on board, went on to open on Broadway in 1998), the number allowed Alan Cumming's sexually charged Emcee to go even further. This late-nineties Emcee was all id, all desire; the suspenders he wore doubled almost as a titillating take on the harness, cupping his crotch so audiences couldn't well ignore it. In Cumming's hands, "Two Ladies" became an even more explicit ode to sexual (and domestic) promiscuity (indeed, one of the Kit Kat Club dancers who joined him for the number was a boy in drag, further muddying the freewheeling sexual prowess of the show's central figure). Cumming's modern Emcee was figured as a hedonist all too happy to grope and grind against his bedfellows and made some of the song's lyrics (like the suggestion there's room at the bottom if you drop in some night) even racier than they'd been already in the hands of Grey all those decades earlier. The Oscar-winning Bob Fosse film gestured toward the sexual perversion that was all the rage in Berlin; its late twentieth-century stage-bound iteration made you feel like you were being welcomed into the city's underground subculture.

There's a joyousness to the number in its embrace of such a deliciously delectable arrangement. Twosies would seem to beat onesies, the Emcee and his "Two Ladies" sing. But nothing, truly, could beat threes! In the film, such lyrics serve also as running commentary on the failed throuple Sally, Brian Roberts (the Cliff character, here a Brit), and playboy Maximilian von Heune haphazardly (and unknowingly) create with one another. Liza Minnelli's Sally, who initially seems taken with shy Brian (Michael York), eventually seduces him despite his protestations that all his previous attempts to bed women have been failures. But once the two begin running in Max's circles (Max, whose wife is, we're told, perfectly okay with him gallivanting and doing his own thing in Berlin), it's clear this makeshift trio is bound to dredge up hurt emotions all around. The film tees off their drunken endeavors with that "Two Ladies" number back at the Kit Kat Club. It's right after that song where we see how one night they all dance and make out together, hinting at the threelationship they could dream of having but never quite commit to in the harsh light of day. But no amount of sultry eyes between these three is enough to have them rise above the petty jealousies that eventually fell them. "You two bastards!" Sally yells at Brian when he confesses to having been sleeping with Max, just as she had been doing behind *his* back. "Shouldn't that be *three*?" he fires back as he exits their quarters.

The Weimar Republic that had dazzled Isherwood in his youth, and which he tried to capture in his writings, nudged him to better embrace his sexuality. In turn, he pushed his readers to think similarly beyond convention when depicting that 1920s European city. As he put it in his memoir, *Christopher and His Kind*, "Here, screaming boys in drag and monocled, Eton-cropped girls in dinner-jackets play-acted the high jinks of Sodom and Gomorrah, horrifying the onlookers and reassuring them that Berlin was still the most decadent city in Europe." Berlin was alive, a kinetic powder keg that played an apt backdrop for the world of those wishing to live a life beyond that which is before them. That's the tragedy of Sally, who's torn between the idyllic image of domestic bliss Brian offers her when she learns she's pregnant (with his or Max's baby, it's unclear), and with the more bohemian life she's grown accustomed to. She chooses the latter, of course, closing out the film extolling the virtues of life as a cabaret, a performance Minnelli delivers with wistful melancholy, egging us to join her at the cabaret that is life, in the process becoming a symbol for a dying (if not outright rotting) world where everything and everyone was possible. And while Isherwood's characters eventually got away from him, becoming cultural touchstones in their own right with only passing resemblance to the people he'd first drawn from in his semi-autobiographical tales, it's fascinating to see that a queer man's writerly exploits gave way for such a funny if fleeting portrait of nontraditional intimacies. The kind that were quite common within the circles Isherwood himself moved in.

The *Goodbye to Berlin* and *A Single Man* writer was a close acquaintance of arguably two of the most famous romantic and artistic triads in early and mid-twentieth-century America: Glenway Wescott, Monroe Wheeler, and George Platt Lynes on one side, and Paul Cadmus, Jared French, and Margaret French (née Hoening) on the other. The former's torrid decades-long intimacies have been chronicled both in Wescott's published private musings (*Continual Lessons: The Journals of Glenway Wescott, 1937–1955*) and in an aptly titled photo travelogue book (*When We Were Three: The Travel Albums of George Platt Lynes, Monroe Wheeler, and Glenway Wescott, 1925–1935*), while the latter's closeness has been immortalized both in their respective art pieces as well as in their joint artistic venture, PaJaMa, which is what they called themselves collectively from the late 1930s into the 1950s, when taking playful photos of themselves and their friends during beachside sojourns in Fire Island

and Provincetown. Both, it must be noted, began with two, with a couple folding in a third with seemingly little regard for what convention and tradition dictated. Moreover, each throuple avant la lettre was a porous proposition, with various other lovers and close acquaintances coming in and out of the lives of the core threesomes at hand.

Paul Cadmus's lustful admiration for Jared French was first and best captured in his 1931 oil painting *Jerry*. Finished during a joint European journey, a few years after the two had met in 1926, the portrait finds French shirtless on a tousled, unmade bed. Cadmus's brushstrokes lovingly contour his partner's muscled torso as well as his handsome facial features (including his short blond curls and neatly trimmed mustache, the kind that make "Jerry" feel like a proto Tom of Finland model). His gaze is directly beckoning us, all while his left hand clutches a copy of James Joyce's *Ulysses*, a book that was at the time still banned in the United States for its "obscene" content. The piece is a provocation, a lover's portrait that flirts with its viewer and envelops him (for it is truly a "him" to which it is addressed) in a kind of cruising gaze. Cruising, in fact, would soon become central to Cadmus's work, which gleefully depicts scenes where bulging young men openly hunger for one another—including, most famously, his 1934 piece *The Fleet's In!*, which found the artist at the center of a controversy for its portrayal of a queer-coded young man soliciting a sailor.

The free-flowing eroticism of Cadmus's work—my favorite remains *The Bath* (1951), which depicts a welcome homoerotic domesticity with its two figures (one in a bathtub, scrubbing his body; the other standing, in socks, combing his hair, their drying laundry hanging in their shared quarters)—felt of a piece with the way he moved through the world. When he and French met Hoening in 1934 and French decided to marry her a few years later, this didn't really destabilize the relationship between the two men. Indeed, their joint work as PaJaMa (cheekily borrowing the first two letters of their names to create a playful portmanteau for their equally cheeky photography work) is as clear an indication that these three artists didn't feel beholden to any sort of traditional structures. Cadmus would also later find himself involved romantically with figure painter George Tooker while still dating the married French: "I had Jerry in the daytime and George at night," he's famously said to have bragged. Later still, he made a home with his long-standing partner, Jon Anderson, in a house next to that of his sister Fidelma, which kept him near Lincoln Kirstein. The famed arts patron and philanthropist, who had first pursued Paul before making a life with the artist's sister instead, continued to have sex with men throughout his decades-long marriage. These many intertwined tales of interlocking bonds speak all the more forcefully to the way this group of friends and lovers built their own kinds of intimacies, tracing new ways of nurturing bonds in ways both filial and romantic, sexual and artistic.

In a 1997 interview that nudged then ninety-two-year-old Cadmus toward admitting whether his relationship with French (and later with Margaret) could be possible and with such wild abandon at the end of the century, Cadmus was characteristically blunt. He didn't see that much difference, though he admitted, perhaps, it had to do more with the milieu than with the time: "I think artists were much freer than other people. But it just seemed natural for our relationships to survive regardless of the configurations between us." And it is those very configurations that these many talents illustrate in their paintings and photographs from the time.

To peruse the postcard-like photos PaJaMa took over the many beachside summers they spent together and with many friends (including Tooker, but also the trio of Wheeler, Wescott, and Platt Lynes) is to witness a carefree attitude about bodies and desires.

Created for their own amusement, they capture a utopian vision of those many triangulated relationships. In a 1940 photograph no doubt staged by Cadmus and taken by Margaret's Leica camera, as many of them were, author Wescott (facing us, in a tee and high-cut swim trunks) holds close a naked Platt Lynes, who, facing away from us, giving us a good look at his well-sculpted ass, is resting his arms on Wescott and Cadmus (also in trunks and a tee, flexing his arm behind his head). Taken in the dunes of Fire Island, the picture captures a tender intimacy between three; with Wescott's and Cadmus's eyes averted from our gaze, it almost feels like you've caught these men (two of whom were indeed madly in love with a third) in a quiet moment, away from the wary and judgmental eyes of the outside world. This is a triangle not as a site for contested emotions (pulling them in three different directions) but as a solid anchoring figure (the kind where three points achieve a formidable balance). There's solid geometry at work here. A foundation can be laid that exists outside of the usual idea of twos, of couples. Here, three is the magic number, a way to not only better navigate a joint endeavor but to do so away from spaces that would see in such a threesome more trouble than it's worth.

The same can be said for Cadmus's own portrait of his trio of friends: *Stone Blossom: A Conversation Piece* (1939–40). Painted around this same time, it finds the loving throuple illustrated in the titular New Jersey estate where they spent many a leisurely weekend and holiday. Lounging under a tree, Wheeler (then the curator of exhibitions and editor of publications at the MoMA), Wescott (a novelist who would soon be publishing his most well-received novel, 1940's *The Pilgrim Hawk*), and Platt Lynes (whose fashion photography would later make him the toast of New York and Hollywood) are in total repose. Aping the genre of the "conversation piece," which referred to group portraits popularized in eighteenth-century England, Cadmus surrounded his three sub-jects with scattered magazines and publications that spoke to their respective careers. In the portrait, the three men exist in a blissful shared intimacy, their comfort with one another obvious to anyone.

In the picture, it is only Wescott who's fully clothed and on his knees; Wheeler is seated, shirtless, reading a magazine while Platt Lynes is wearing little else but a posing thong while lounging in the grass. Wescott is the observer of the three, his downward gaze admiring Platt Lynes's beautiful half-naked figure. His role as spectator and chronicler was just as true in real life. "Since I can't think when," he writes in a 1937 journal entry, shortly after hanging out with Cadmus, "I have wanted to give some account of myself as a lover and a loved one, of the plot of my life replete with coinci-dences and influences, Monroe's influence especially but not solely, and now of that triumvirate in which I figure in third place, perhaps more governed than governing, who knows?" A few lines later, he reveals that what would become his 1940 novel, *The Pilgrim Hawk: A Love Story*, was in some ways a response to how he was process-ing his current triangular sexual and romantic situation. He writes that he's begun "comparing [Platt Lynes] to a falconer, myself to a falcon." A few days later, he expounds on this metaphor, reaching for it shortly after he remembers how Platt Lynes had told him it was high time he found himself a "new substitute lover." To make sense of what his boyfriend's (newer) boyfriend was asking him, Wescott retreats into his metaphorical menagerie: "So the falconer plucks off the falcon's dark hood," he writes. "But the falcon, blinded by its dream in the darkness, cannot see much; and infatuated with the master's hand upon which it sits, by which in the past it has been fed ideally, it cannot care much." The self-pitying is hard to ignore ("it cannot fly very well," he adds about this metaphorical bird of prey), but it's obvious that the domesticity Wescott had become

accustomed to had somehow weathered his own independence—
his own ability to not just seek prey for himself but to want to crave
it. Namely, even within the privacy of his journals, Wescott can't
escape the way he feels like he's been neutered by the very romance
that had once emboldened him. Where he once could fly and roam
and hunt, here he is now wholly stripped of his wild ways.

It's hard not to read into *The Pilgrim Hawk* the kind of cathar-
tic self-psychologizing of a writer and lover eager to make sense of
the pitfalls of a triangular threelationship. Not just because Wescott
uses his literary alter ego, Alwyn Tower, as his narrator but because
the angled dynamics he narrativizes felt particularly personal.
In the novella, Alwyn is staying with a friend of his in a house on
the outskirts of Paris where, during the course of an afternoon, the
keenly observant novelist meets the Cullens, a piquant Irish couple
who arrive with one other visitor in tow, a hawk-in-training named
Lucy. Alwyn's description of this loud and boorish couple—she's
all bumbling flesh, he's all drunken stupor—makes clear their marriage has been strained by the arrival of Lucy into their lives. *The
Pilgrim Hawk*, riddled with symbolic imagery as it is, carves out
novel ways of telling a story about three, and about the struggles of
wanting to be free and wild when you've been trained to be tame
and domesticated.

In the 1930s and 1940s, Wescott couldn't escape these notions
of what it meant to create new ways of relating—in threes rather
than twos. He didn't have to look too far. As a close friend of Paul
Cadmus, he saw firsthand how another triumvirate navigated such
thorny waters. He was drawn to Cadmus's relationship with Jared
French, curious about how they defied any neat categorization,
with Cadmus allowing his lover to bed many a female lover ("Paul
has admired him all the more for this," Wescott writes) and yet that
never coming in between the bond they shared together. Amid those

same entries where Wescott toys with the helpful notion of seeing himself as a blinded falcon in George's eyes, he expounds on what he witnessed between Cadmus and the new Mr. and Mrs. French. "This spring Jared decided to marry the mistress whom he has loved best," he writes. "Paul doubted whether he could ever be happy again; but now that it is done, I see no indication of tragic disorder." The twinned trios were clearly struggling with how to organize their own romantic arrangements, how to make room for one another without losing sight of what they each wanted. Both Cadmus and Wescott, it seems, had to open up their lives and loves in order to remain wedded to whom they cherished the most, eventually creating a seemingly blissful (though far from perfect) vision of domesticity that organized itself around three.

The following year, as he still worked on *The Pilgrim Hawk*, Wescott would again turn to fiction to wrestle with the added arrangements his own triumvirate rested on. Originally written in 1938, Wescott's short story "A Visit to Priapus" was not published until 2013, close to three decades after the novelist's death. Again making use of his fictional alter ego, Alwyn Tower, Wescott turns his narrative eye unto himself once more. Much as in his life at that point, Alwyn is a sexually frustrated writer who, upon the suggestion of one of his partners (that'd be "George"), has organized a meeting with a stranger, a young and quite hung mediocre painter. When we first meet Alwyn, he's begrudgingly on his way to Maine to meet the well-endowed man who gives the short story its title. As in Wescott's journals, there's a morose tone to the proceedings: "Naturally, bitter regret for my great days as a lover assailed me," Alwyn wonders as he waits for his erstwhile date. "Also a fresh and terrible kind of sense of devotion to the two whom I love, who love me, who cannot keep me happy, whom I torment and disappoint year in and year out, ached in my grotesque heart." That whirlwind of emotions cannily captures what can sometimes be so disorienting about dating two; your anxieties can just as easily be halved as they can be doubled, making you feel twice as self-conscious and half as confident about how and what you feel on any given day. All the more reason to not allow either to be forced to satisfy your every need.

Alwyn has driven himself to meet this unknown fellow because he feels, as Wescott did in real life, that he should be able to find sexual satisfaction outside of his own threelationship. Platt Lynes and Wheeler did so seemingly with no qualms. Why shouldn't Wescott? Why shouldn't Alwyn? The rendezvous is mostly a disaster, a comedy of shameful and shame-driven errors that find neither man able to handily pleasure the other during what seems like an interminable night together at a rural inn in Maine. In the young Priapus's touch, Alwyn could constantly feel him thinking: "Thinking, thinking, explaining himself a little, at least to himself; justifying himself a little, or trying to decide how to go about justifying himself if he should have to; and resenting little things I did or things I said, but losing track of his resentment at once, all absorbed in some sort of theory of love, or policy of being my lover, or dubious general scheme of loveableness." Wescott's narrator is akin to my own inner voice, to the narrator in my head who cannot get out of his way even in moments of intense sexual intimacy. And throughout this short story, the Midwestern writer puts us squarely in the mind of his alter ego, a man so afflicted by a crippling self-consciousness he cannot even let himself enjoy a romp with a hung stranger without pursuing any number of intellectual detours into what men like him (or like his makeshift partner for the night) make of encounters like these. Alwyn goes back and forth between being sincere in his lust for that not-so-great hung painter and recognizing how much those kinds of hook-ups depend on posturing; between being open and vulnerable and being cunning and calculating. All of this is wrapped around the perils of having such a monstrous tool ("more troubled than troublesome—like the sex of some shy wild animal") but anchored, as well, in what two strangers map out for each other when agreeing to meet once and nevermore. Do you ache for love in that moment or merely lust? Do you playact a familiar kind of intimacy or inch your way toward it? Or do you, as Alwyn does, spend the entirety of it creating a neat narrative on which to project any and all the insecurities you have about such trysts?

At the end of the day, such a meeting is an excuse for Alwyn/ Wescott to tease out what it is he wanted out of life, out of love, out of sex. More of a confessional self-examination than its titillating title might suggest, "A Visit to Priapus" ends up serving as a lesson in what trysts with strangers can proffer you. For, after reflecting on this most unsuccessful of hookups, Alwyn recognizes just how fortunate he is to love and care for two while also being able to satiate his needs elsewhere if need be. And such an episode had granted him respite precisely because it would have no future: "I hoped and prayed that I might never need to see him again: to that extent the present need had been attended to," he writes toward the end of this sardonic tale.

Wescott was clearly sorting through the way the many lovers and crushes and hookups he and Wheeler and Platt Lynes would have over the decades to come would nurture rather than rupture their own arrangement. Here was a fictional attempt at experimenting with openness: rather than leash themselves to one another, keeping their wild and unruly desires under falcon hoods, they egged one another to hunt for prey when and if they needed— all while still knowing said forays would bring them back into each other's arms with perhaps a stronger sense of stability—the kind of wholeness *Detransition, Baby*'s Ames wishes for, the kind *Passages*'s Tomas fumbles into.

Wescott's writings feel like missives from a distant past that nevertheless feel remarkably modern. His apprehension over finding solace in other people's beds, both in sudden trysts and in more long-standing affairs, echoes the many anxieties I've come to experience as I learned how to situate myself anew within a porous threesome. Here is a fictional—and also a very *real*—world built on *ands* not on *ors*. On a free-flowing sense of eroticism that suffuses intimacies both close and further afield. Which is not to say this trio was without its faults or its follies; Wescott doesn't hide just how difficult it was, at times, to feel like a third wheel. Or how feeling unwanted by his partners (or even casual hookups) affected his own self-worth. Though he wouldn't have used a word like *polyamory*—or even *consensual nonmonogamy*—Wescott was committed to breaking through traditional expectations. Prompted by decades' worth of sexual and romantic intimacies with men other than Wheeler, in 1952 Wescott wrote candidly in his journals about his vexed investment in "old fashioned love relationships in binary form." While he was clearly a romantic, he had come to the conclusion that "for most males the two-person pattern is just an ideal, an imposed discipline, a convention, a hypocrisy, a phase or episode; and that especially in homosexuality, that is, in double maleness, everything that may come under the heading of an imitation of male and female romanticism is rather short-lived, one-sided, anguished, laborious, wearisome." He was diagnosing—a tad too broadly, no doubt—the way twosomes have long been defined and exalted by the world around us, leaving little room for the kinds of arrangements he and Wheeler (and Platt Lynes) had built over the years. Companionship and commitment he saw all around him. And he valued it, in turn.

"But as a rule, if you look close," he cautioned and comforted himself, "not in simple duality."

10.
STRANGER

"HELLO, STRANGER."

As a closer, you really can't ask for a more disorienting pair of words. If as an opener this was a tantalizing provocation, asking us to imagine how, why—and crucially, to whom—one would address such a line, framing it as a closing sentiment should have us wonder what kind of estrangement and familiarity we've upended in the process. A stranger would presumably be one no more toward the end of any kind of interaction. You'd only utter such a greeting now to further establish how that pull toward closeness, toward intimacy, exists no more. Or has failed, perhaps. Whatever move toward a narrative, wherein you would come to know them better, has fractured and proved too facile. Whatever winking knowingness was there at the start has likely soured into a wry resolution. No longer a come-on but an ironic goodbye, we may find ourselves with a formulation that reminds us how every ending is but another beginning, and maybe how some beginnings can only be marked alongside twinned ends.

Closer closes its threaded tale of love and betrayal with the same song and images that open it. A young woman is walking through the crowded streets of a city as Damien Rice's "The Blower's Daughter" thunders all around us. Her unguarded beauty remains striking as she makes her way through the crowd. In the opening scene, she catches the eye of a young man across the street, the only Good Samaritan who'll help her when she's struck by a cabbie in London, distracted as she was by that handsome lad in front of her then. "Hello, stranger," she'd uttered as her eyes alighted on him (on us), opening out into a flirty conversation that would set the tone for Patrick Marber's cruel journey through modern dating in Mike Nichols's 2004 film. In the final scene, we're nudged to think the young woman (played by Natalie Portman) will say those words again, only to someone else. Or, better yet, we've come to realize that those two words served less as a provocative introduction than as a distancing confession. As we learn, she hadn't really allowed herself to be known. She'd lied about her name, perhaps even about her entire backstory (Marber's play is much more explicit about this). In the end, as she walks through the streets in Manhattan, she's unshackled herself from the life she had back in London. The bloke she met there has been left to pick up the pieces of his life alone; with one final reveal, she turns herself, with but a few words, into an estranged partner.

The thrill of meeting and making a connection with a stranger is rooted in the endless possibilities they open for us. But the loss of someone whose familiarity has helped erect the life you inhabit can be just as dizzying. Not someone who's a stranger but someone who will become one. That is what is most affecting about a breakup, about a divorce. You get to watch, in real time, how someone you knew intimately becomes an unfamiliar being almost overnight. The inside jokes erode into nothing. The physical cues evaporate on sight. The person whose moods you could read like the weather is suddenly gone; all the data you've accumulated over years is suddenly obsolete. Useless, even. To grieve for such a loss is to grieve for what you had. But also to grieve for yourself, for the person you were for and with and maybe even because of the other.

This was, I'll admit, the hardest part about coming to terms with my own divorce. And was why I had, as I'd done so many times before, turned to *Closer* for comfort. But such emotional cutting, as a friend termed it, kept ringing ever hollower the more I revisited Marber's quartet of cheating liars who continually egg on one another to leave their lives behind and start with them anew ("*I'm* your stranger," one character tells another. "Jump!"). Maybe this isn't a film about the fun act of flirtation, about reveling in the possibilities of meeting strangers, about the exciting ways you can find yourself in someone else over and over again ("If you believe in love at first sight, you never stop looking" was the film's tagline). Maybe it is, instead, a piece about how the search to be seen and loved and desired and coveted and pursued *solely by* strangers is (and will always be) a futile way to maintain any semblance of a coherent self. There's the crux of how much stock we put into our romantic relationships—in the myth of a loving couple. We are to be known by someone, by some *one*, intimately.

The very act of dating two has required a reorientation of how I understand intimacy. It's required, for instance, constantly needing to pluralize such a concept. Just as we've had to embrace the many intersecting and at times overlapping *we*'s that make up our relationship, I've found myself having to conceptualize an expansive sense of the many equally intricate intimacies we nurture in and around one another. This comes not just from the mere act of dating two, but of dating two while eschewing sexual exclusivity between us three. Such an arrangement—which I'll admit has proven to be as exciting, though not, for that, any less emotionally taxing, than I'd always imagined it would be—rests on our shared commitment to openness.

Openness does not come easily to me. Even in a book that requires certain disclosures, I can feel my reticence toward revealing too much of myself and allowing others in. I find myself reaching for euphemisms and metaphors, for obscure historical concepts and far-flung artistic avatars to avoid making it read like a diaristic confession (or a confessional diary). For years, I told myself that I needed to be closed off emotionally (and sexually too, I guess) out of a desire to feel safe. Coming of age in the nineties made any inkling of same-sex desire feel tinged with fear. And later I came to find that there were parts of myself so rooted and rotted in shame that I couldn't find healthy ways to let them bloom in daylight. I locked them inside instead, deep within me where they could never be witnessed by others, especially those whose love and companionship I so craved. They were never too far gone, though, having been shuttled deep within my phone, that repository of my deepest, most shameful wants. Soon they ivied themselves around flirty DMs and NSFW sexting exchanges, and grew in darkness with every new salacious thirst trap I took and sent and encouraged others to send back. Such compartmentalizing came at quite the high cost. It's why, since I needed to start anew as a divorcé inching toward his fortieth birthday, I realized I owed it to myself to be known. Wholly. To others and also to myself. It meant confronting what it is I really wanted, embracing an openness that's as much sexual as it is emotional.

One of the greatest joys of this threelantionship has been the mutual, if hard-won, encouragement to see our openness as a central pillar of how we care for one another. We've done so at orgies in Palm Springs and at cruising bars in Madrid, in back rooms in Mexico City and sex clubs in London. I could talk about the panic

attacks I've had at some of these spaces or the jealous fits I've unwittingly unleashed at others, but what I keep trying to take away
from each of those moments is the potential for finding a shared
desire that's not limited but expansive.

There has not been a better distillation of our shared hedo-
nistic impulses than the many hours we've spent together (or at
least in the same room) while in the safe haven of the aptly titled
Burning Man camp Comfort & Joy. Amid a weeklong celebration
that exalts participation, immediacy, and radical self-expression,
the queer camp of Comfort & Joy—which is mostly based out of
San Francisco—bristles with the bacchanalian promise that this
desert-set festival-cum-community-driven-experience is so well
known (and oft mocked) for. One of Burning Man's ten principles,
after all, is Radical Inclusion ("Anyone may be a part of Burning
Man. We welcome and respect the stranger," as cofounder Larry
Harvey once put it), and the Afterglow tent at Comfort & Joy is designed as a space where you can indulge in any and every lustful desire you may harbor, with whichever stranger you may so covet. In
the camp's own words, the Afterglow is "a different kind of haven—
shrouded by dayglo flags, beckoning with promises of unhindered
self expression and interpersonal exploration, this 24/7 space is an
open invitation to all seeking respite from the boisterous festivities
of the playa taking time to indulge their wildest desires . . . or simply observe + unwind, at will. This is a safe space held for queer
immediacy, self-definition and respect." It feels trite but true to say
the time spent at Afterglow and Comfort & Joy has been reduced
to a blur of bodies and limbs and kisses and caresses and the like, a
puddle of sweat-tinged skin hungering for desires there at the ready.

Yes, those hours spent at Comfort & Joy felt like a sex-crazed
fantasy come to life. But my mind didn't immediately go to porn
(mostly because I'm that rare breed of red-blooded homosexual who

spends almost no time browsing sites or Twitter alts or OnlyFans accounts in his spare time). My thoughts went instead, snob of a cinephile that I am, to *Shortbus*. That 2006 John Cameron Mitchell film, after all, owes much of its queered sensibility to the Radical Faeries and various artistic collectives in the downtown New York City scene (including Stephen Kent Jusick's MIX screening series) that feel of a piece with the eroticized spaces of communion and community like Comfort & Joy. And the film, which opens with a gay couple hoping to get advice from a therapist as to how best to open their relationship, and ends with a raucous, sensuous orgy at its eponymous downtown party in the middle of the Northeast blackout in 2003, is best remembered now as that rare U.S. film to feature unsimulated sex. And while such scenes remain eyebrow-raising close to two decades later (you've never seen a threesome quite like the one depicted in the film, featuring as it does the U.S. anthem sung into someone's asshole), the spirit of the project was not about sex but sexuality. About sensuous connections, not sexual acrobatics. Its many sex scenes—including those that take place at the Shortbus salon in between film screenings and makeshift consciousness-raising conversations—function the same way songs do in musicals. They both punctuate and advance the plot. They reveal deep-seated character details that would otherwise have been hard to unearth. This is a film, after all, that's anchored by a pre-orgasmic woman searching her way toward that most ecstatic of short-lived moments.

The many intersecting plots that make up *Shortbus* feel novel and refreshing precisely because they do away with familiar narratives. The finalized script was developed over several years and a few intense months of casting, improvisation, and workshopping with the actors Mitchell eventually invited onto the project (to audition, all performers first had to send a video of themselves talking about "a true-life sexual experience that was very important" to them). Such an unorthodox and intensely collaborative endeavor resulted in a film that depicted and mirrored the gathering space that gives it its name. "You've heard of the Big Yellow School Bus?" Justin Vivian Bond's Mistress of Shortbus explains. "Well, this is the short one. It's a salon for the gifted and challenged." The downtown space, which is equal parts performance site and sex party venue, welcomes all who wish to find a place to belong. Neither dispelling nor outright dismissing the centrality of sexual intimacy to our everyday lives, *Shortbus* demands we recognize the ways sex can connect us to others, yes, but also to ourselves. A couple come together with the help of a prying, voyeuristic neighbor and a flirty third they invite into their bedroom; meanwhile, a tough-on-the-outside but tender-on-the-inside dominatrix ends up helping two halves of a couple, the sex therapist who's been faking her orgasms and the boyfriend who's been hiding his bondage kinks from her. Mitchell and his characters preach a kind of openness that values collectivity, the kind the filmmaker developed behind and in front of the camera.

One of my favorite details about *Shortbus* has little to do with its threaded tales about a post-9/11 New York City. Or, in fact, it's the way the film makes the famed city feel small and intimate, reclaiming it away from the imagery of piercing headlines and ravaged footage that had so defined it in the years following those terrorist attacks. Rather than using establishing shots, Mitchell's camera zeroes into the many rooms and spaces the film takes place in by zooming in and out of a handcrafted replica of the city's many towering buildings. Akin to a fifth grader's maquette of the Big Apple, the New York City of *Shortbus* looks like a Play-Doh set fit for the playful tales its many windows hold.

In spirit it recalls the worlds Ned Asta drew for Larry Mitchell's dreamy 1977 novel, *The Faggots & Their Friends Between Revolutions.*

Their illustrated collaboration imagines a queer geography where faeries, faggots, queens, and their many allies live in harmony with one another and see themselves as fighting the drab world of men. Borrowing from feminist and Marxist thought, much like the Lavender Hill commune the writer and artist belonged to in the late 1960s and 1970s, *The Faggots & Their Friends Between Revolutions* weaves a cheeky mythology where a group of friends who call themselves the Tribe of the Rising Sons first move into a house and make it their own: they paint it pink (the trim lavender, obviously), carve peacock feathers into the wood around the door, and even plant roses in the backyard. Soon they realize the entire neighborhood is filled with similar communities and collectives. All around them are spaces like the Horney Heaven replete with the Faggot Fuck Palace (home of the House of the Heavy, Horney Hunks) and Elegant City (where the bourgeois rituals of old are pursued); groups like the Gay as a Goose Tribe, the Boys in the Back Room, and the No-Name Tribe have each created environments that befit their given monikers. In a two-page spread that precedes the various descriptions of these houses, Asta produced one of their signature Aubrey Beardsley–inspired illustrations of this imaginary city that looks not unlike the New York skyline depicted in *Shortbus*. These buildings, some of which boast lips and eyes (in addition to keyholes and moons for windows), are branded with words ("FAGGOT" some windows spell; "DYKE" runs down a building's facade). Together they give Asta's bustling, black-and-white sketched city a surrealist tenor that makes this two-dimensional drawing feel like it's pulsating with anarchic energy.

Larry Mitchell's description of this budding faggot world is intentionally utopian (like that of John Cameron Mitchell's own *Shortbus*). In the late 1970s, it was imperative to dream up such spaces, to imagine welcoming environments that illustrated the emboldening unity that could come from living outside of the straining strictures of patriarchal society. It's fitting that Mitchell (Larry, that is, though John Cameron too) grounds his fag lore novel not (just) on couples but on collectives—on communities and nonnormative groupings that by their very geometry and organization defy neat categorization. Take the tribe of Angel Flesh, which lives next door to the Tribe of the Rising Sons. Their house is devoted to various living forms (one room is "filled with velvets and feathers and make-up and sparkles and costumes and silks. It is where the faggots go when they want to transform themselves"). More importantly, though, Mitchell notes that all who live in the house of Angel Flesh "have given to all the others complete access to each other's body." Theirs is a world rooted in porousness: "Each night in the big central room of the house, when sleep comes, they hold each other until they hardly know where one of them stops and another one begins." This is intimacy as a new way to remove the boundaries we erect around ourselves. Between me and you. Between us and the world. This dissolution is framed as utopian, as an aspirational image where communion between friends is a powerful rebuke to the insidious call toward individuation Mitchell so observes in the world of men.

Presenting *Shortbus* to a crowd in Portland during the film's much-anticipated 2022 rerelease (its first ever), Mitchell urged viewers to take what they were about to see in stride. "Have a great time," he said. "Suspend not just your disbelief but your beliefs, and again, like a relationship, we frontload it with sex. By the end, it's cuddles all around." This was, in fact, what the movie's original U.S. poster promised. Featuring the film's entire cast (clothed, one must add) shot from up above, the promo staged a group photo where everyone's tangled limbs and bodies exuded a joyous buoyancy seen most explicitly in everyone's gleefully giggling expressions. Anticipating the way sex would be top of everyone's minds when seeking out the film, the poster aimed for a softened approach, only nudging toward the movie's more salacious sensibility in its cheeky pun-laden tagline ("You've got to get on to get off"). But given the film's narrative edges toward an all-out embrace of cuddling as a site of healing and exploration, of comfort and joy, the marketing team's decision to stage a cuddle puddle to sell this quirky flesh-fueled tale was a canny one. Not only did it push back against the sensationalism that would have otherwise defined the film's reception. But it amplified, instead, the coy collaborative sensibility Mitchell brought to bear with his carefully curated cast and crew. *Shortbus* was a call toward embracing the very pleasures of such embraces, the ones you share with partners, with hook-ups, and yes, even with friends.

Months before *Shortbus* premiered at the 2006 Cannes Film Festival, *New York Magazine* published an article titled "The Cuddle Puddle of Stuyvesant High School" (its headline in the cover was slightly more sensationalist, egging you on to consider "Love and the Ambisexual Heteroflexible Teen"). Alex Morris's piece focused on a group of school-aged teens in New York City who spent their free tenth period every day in what they termed a "cuddle puddle" where there was always "girls petting girls and girls petting guys and guys petting guys." For Morris, this decidedly small sample size of a population in an already rarified high school space (Stuyvesant has an admissions rate of 3 percent) nevertheless served as an example of a changing understanding of sexuality on the part of a younger generation who was letting go of needless labels and strictures. And embracing, in turn, a fluid approach to their ever-flowing desires.

The cuddle puddle served as an obvious instantiation of this. Here was an image that immediately broke apart any neat ideas about how intimacies could be embodied, let alone codified. Unlike a hug or a kiss, which are passing and rarely require more than two people, a cuddle puddle thrives on comforting chaos. You cuddle with or around someone when you care for them and want to feel held or want to hold them in return. To do so in a puddle of others is to forgo any one direction in which your attention—be it intimate or erotic—is channeled. Morris himself was overwhelmed by the very geometry Stuyvesant's "cuddle puddle" called for: "It practically takes a diagram to plot all the various hookups and connections within [it]," he told his readers. Indeed, the cuddle puddle all but demands you fail when trying to map out the many ways in which these teenagers were connecting with one another. And in his attempt to do so (however imperfectly) Morris missed the point of this kind of grouping, of this kind of physical closeness. The kind that does away with the lines between flirting and hooking up and stands as a kind of blurred area between petting and hugging, between kissing and making out, and yet could somehow involve any and all of the above. Perhaps this is why I'm so enthralled with it as a figure of intimacy, because of its elusive yet self-explanatory nature. (Self-explanatory to English speakers, at least; Spanish doesn't really have a comparable term. Which is why a close friend of mine who hails from Mexico would occasionally say he wanted to "smuggle" with someone, so foreign was the concept in his vocabulary.)

To lose yourself in a cuddle puddle—as the faggots and their friends do, as the many Shortbus visitors enjoyed doing, and as the Stuyvesant kids clearly embraced—is to yearn for a kind of bodily connection that can straddle the line between the chaste and the erotic. One that can lead into more but can just as easily satisfy you if you're intimately famished. As the Stuyvesant kids show (and as *Shortbus* and *The Faggots & Their Friends Between Revolutions* remind us), cuddling can be a rather public act that rests on a tender, more private form of intimacy. In his playfully titled book *The Cuddle Sutra: An Unabashed Celebration of the Ultimate Intimacy*, author Rob Grader tries to do the opposite, wrestling cuddling away from such casual openness and into the very language many have reserved for sexual encounters. "Let's face it," he writes with the grating earnestness so common in these self-help books, all of which root their insights in the language of self-evident and therefore unequivocal truths, "we can have sex with someone without meaning much, but it is pretty close to impossible to enjoy some casual cuddling. In fact, it may well be the best test of whether or not that person in your bed is the right one for you." There's a winking irony (I hope) in saying this within the pages of a book that riffs on the world's most well-known erotic how-to manual. But Grader's language puts him squarely within the confines of the couple in the bedroom, that mythic place reserved for "the one." Cuddling, I won't deny, is quite an intimate way to show affection toward someone else. But, like sex itself (in any and all its variations), it need not become hallowed ground between two—let alone two presuming to be one. By its very wording, a *cuddle puddle* does away with such limitations, calling forth images of a natural occurrence that depends on free-flowing spillage. By its very imagery, a cuddle puddle demands you think of its elements as getting lost in the whole, limbs and torsos blending and bleeding into one another with gentle ease.

The contemporary artist who best exemplifies the emotional and aesthetic promises of such a "puddle" is Salman Toor. The Lahore-born and New York City–based figurative painter has slowly begun amassing a budding collection of pieces titled *Fag Puddle* that very clearly plays with a desire to coalesce bodies, limbs, lovers, and objects in a kind of queer, green-hued surrealist space—one made all the more viscous and visceral by Toor's own vividly impressed brushstrokes that give a plunging vibrancy to his work. Toor, who originally was drawn to the great European masters and honed his style by emulating their fastidious focus on color, composition, and scene-making, has over the past few years begun to experiment with a much freer approach. One that balances his desire for realism with a newer penchant for irreverence. For surprise. For the kind of passing scenes he keeps being drawn to (friends lounging or dancing or hugging, at bars, in cabs, in beds). The result is a stirring sensibility that's grounded in haziness, in clouded meanings that aim to be more associative than descriptive. There's a strangeness to them. One that's beckoning rather than alienating. Ambika Trasi, the curatorial assistant at the Whitney Museum who'd first followed his work and who played a pivotal part in mounting the artist's *How Will I Know* exhibit at the museum in the spring of 2020, explained to *The New Yorker* that she'd found Toor's oil paintings quite evocative of the equally alienating and community-driven life many make for themselves in New York City: "There was an intimacy about them that I hadn't seen before," she added.

That seemingly unseen intimacy has cemented Toor, alongside fellow artists (and some even close friends) like Doron Langberg, Louis Fratino, Kyle Coniglio, and Anthony Cudahy, as part of a new wave of figure portraitists dubbed the New Queer Intimists. These young artists (my contemporaries, as it turns out) insist on a porousness between subjects and their surroundings. But also on a porousness between the various kinds of intimacies they illustrate. You see it in a painting like Toor's *Three Friends in a Cab* (2021), where a whirring New York City landscape plays backdrop to a cozy taxi ride between three boys whose bodies are intertwined in the back seat as they head out to (or back from) a delightful night together. Or in works like *Downtown Boys* (2020), *Dancing to Whitney* (2018), and *Afterparty* (2019), all of which depict scenes of affection between friends in enclosed homey spaces—some even hinting at more sexual closeness between not just two but perhaps even three. Toor's paintings risk spilling out of their frames and enveloping us with their intoxicating absinthe-like candor.

In this he shares a sensibility with fellow Queer Intimist and friend Doron Langberg. The two have long seen their careers incessantly intersect, what with their shared interest in the Dutch masters and a penchant for a contemporary vision of queer portraiture. In spring 2021, Langberg and Toor were featured together in *T* magazine's "With Friends" cover story as examples of friends-as-muses. And by that fall, the portraits they'd sketched of each other were a part of Luhring Augustine's *Plus One* exhibit, which celebrated interpersonal relationships and community building within and across the art world in New York City. Like Toor's work, Langberg's encourages us to see the world intimately. Not just the world, but *their* world. With their focus on their everyday experiences, on depicting domestic interiors, and recognizing in them a wide-ranging exploration of queer life, Toor and Langberg welcome their viewers into a private life that's made public, a way to understand their lives through the subjective gaze they cast upon them. In an essay that hoped to locate Langberg in conversation with the Intimists of the late nineteenth and twentieth century, Tyler Malone stresses how much the Israeli-born figurative artist suffused his paintings with the interiority they hoped to capture. There's a permeable, palpable line that's blurred between his subjects and the spaces they inhabit, with hazed colors and softened brushstrokes edging us to never think of them as distinct. "The spaces should feel like emotional spaces," Langberg told Malone. "Obviously they exist as inhabitable spaces—I want the viewer to feel that it's a real space that they could enter into—but also something that's more of a continuation of the figure's interior life."

In addition to the domesticity that often characterizes Toor's work, he's drawn, as well, to encounters between seeming strangers. Yet those encounters feel weighted with an erotic—with an *intimate*—pull that further muddles such neat distinctions between what's known and who's unknown, between who's familiar and what's been estranged. Toor's lines and colors aim constantly to bridge and muddle gaps between time and space, between art historical pasts and vibrant queer presents. With *The Bar on East 13th* (2019), for example, Toor has taken inspiration from Édouard Manet's 1882 portrait *A Bar at the Folies-Bergère* to create a modern, coy interaction not between a lily-white barmaid and a mustachioed gentleman in a Paris nightclub but between a long-haired bartender and a presumably queer Brown guy in a Manhattan bar whose disco ball tinges Toor's signature green hues with flashes of light in its background. The gazes exchanged between the two boys are somewhat inscrutable. There's a hint of something between them, a wry knowingness that etches itself at the edge of their expressions, perhaps made all the more legible by the convivial atmosphere of the bar around them (a young couple is embracing and making out to the right of them). Just as in Manet's portrait, here is an inviting gaze that urges us to inch forward, to take in the image presented and the reflection there encased (it's a mirror behind the bartender that is giving us a look at Toor's other main subject, who's seen only in said reflection). The two boys may be strangers but Toor has forever bound them into an intimacy that, in turn, envelops those of us who are welcomed to witness it whenever our eyes land on them.

This is also the case in two other pieces that somewhat echo each other: *Art Room* (2020) and *Museum Boys* (2021). Each stages a happenstance meeting between two boys who, perhaps, see in the other's gaze a thrilling (new?) way to look at themselves, the room around them, and the art they now inhabit and call forth with their own presence. Each scene takes place at a gallery of sorts where art historical artifacts dot the environment, with one of Toor's signature "fag puddles" serving as a centerpiece, a recursive instantiation of the artist's desire to bring his own artistry into the hallowed halls where masters like Manet, for instance, have long belonged. *Museum Boys*, commissioned by the Frick Collection, was created to sit in the space left empty by one of the museum's most prized paintings, Johannes Vermeer's *Officer and Laughing Girl* (1657): whatever Toor created would be indebted to but also in conversation with that famed oil painting, which depicts a curious interaction between an officer and a ruefully smiling girl, a merchant's map on the wall serving as their backdrop. The final piece was less an imitation or even a response to Vermeer; it was a reworking of the Dutch master's sensibility through a queer modern lens. Toor's green hues again dominate the oil painting where a pants-less Brown young man (sporting what looks like a clownish nose, a pink dot over his face, a Vermeeresque red-feathered hat in one hand, and only one sneaker on his right foot) and a blond figure, equally disrobed (both, disavowing the need for pants, it seems), stare at a vitrine that stands between them. There, Toor has assembled two tangled naked male bodies alongside a Cinderella heel, a Duchamp urinal, a small bottle (of poppers, perhaps?), a rag, and a condom—a fag puddle as erotically charged as you can devise, perhaps the better to help frame these "Museum Boys" as doing more than merely observing the art around them. Yet there's a tenderness to the entire scene, both inside and outside the vitrine.

As Xavier F. Salomon writes of *Museum Boys* in *Living Histories: Queer Views and Old Masters*, "Toor's work always encourages close looking and interpretation. It urges the acceptance of a mood and a feeling, embracing what is before our eyes and letting our imaginations connect the dots." The focal point of the painting is that fag puddle in the vitrine, which seems as intriguing to Toor's painted figures as it is to us: we're encouraged to look closer, to look more deeply and with more curiosity at the various objects and body parts Toor has so perfectly strewn on-site for us—many of which are decidedly familiar but have been made to look more playfully out of place because of it. Toor's various *Fag Puddle* pieces began with *Parts and Things* (2019). Awash in Toor's signature jade green (a color as noxious as it is joyous), the still life riff features an open coat closet, illuminated by a single bare light bulb. The mound of "parts and things" it depicts includes a pink feathered boa wrapped around many boys' torsos, heads, and limbs, which are severed, yes, but not with violence (there's no blood here, only sculptural bodily pieces). They're jumbled and scattered all over one another as if they'd been strewn there on purpose. "I think of these fag puddles as heaps of exhaustion and lust," he's said. "And they're usually kind of leaky. It's just a bunch of things that I'm thinking about that I turn into this kind of pathetic and funny heap."

Toor's "fag puddles" are by definition unruly and expansive; they're an instantiation of more is more, of lives and bodies and objects gathered haphazardly but invitingly as well. They make you want to not figure out what took place but to take its place, to enter into their cozied, lustful spaces. Later, his titles would be more informative about what these mountains of "parts and things" were. In 2022's *Fag Puddle with Candle, Shoe, and Flag*, Toor yet again has depicted a green-tinged bric-a-brac assemblage where a striped tie, a shoe, a belt, a blond boy's head, a naked boy's ass, and a hand holding a mace (among many other figural details) are carefully arranged in front of a tripod with a smartphone on it whose flash has only just gone off. As with 2020's *Fag Puddle with Pearls and Sock and Shrubs*, Toor cannot escape the latent eroticism of his titles: the bare though furred asses he sketches seem primed to be rimmed or fucked, and even when his dicks and bodies lie limp, their languid poses capture that feeling of postcoital bliss. It makes sense he keeps making room for such expressions of queer male intimacy in his paintings—especially the ones, like *Museum Boys* and *Art Room* that call up the institutional spaces that have for so long kept such open expressions of unburdened desire out of our artistic purview. The leakages Toor so beautifully explores and contours in his work are a call away from older, more rigid models of being and seeing. There's a breakage here—a leakage, as he puts it—of borders and limits, an openness toward a different way of connecting with one another and with the world around us. There's a function to all those mirrors Toor paints for us. He knows our gaze into his world will undoubtedly reflect back at us more than we've bargained for.

Toor's paintings—like Frank O'Hara's poetry or Peter Hujar's photographs, though in a decidedly different register—call forth that Sondheimian vision of *ands* not *ors*. His vision of "fag puddles" is one that dreams up intimate scenes of collapsing interiorities, their porousness blending bodies and spaces into playful ideas of company and companionship. They defy narratives precisely because they capture a moment suspended in time, though one that honeys itself into an artistic morass where time will always stand still, calling us to remember what such moments in our own lives may look like when we wish to melt into the bodies or spaces around us. When, like *Closer*'s Alice, we may wish to blend in with the crowd the better to escape a life left behind and imagine a newer one ahead.

I've kept wanting to get lost in such moments where I search for potential connections, for possible contacts, if we must use

Samuel R. Delany's more pliant wording. Moments where I can be called to be any of my many selves by a mere lustful glance or an inviting look that simultaneously pulls me in and out of myself. I've found it happen in quiet moments with my boyfriends while at home (it can be dizzying to have such twinned gazes bear witness to your life) and in ecstatic ones amid larger crowds (where the fine line between you and other, be it on the dance floor, in a back room, at a Burning Man camp, or a nudist gathering, can feel fluid and flowing). And so I've arrived precisely where I started, suspended in a moment in time looking at someone who feels alien and familiar in equal measure. Someone I feel like I've known my whole life yet who's finally revealing themselves to me as if for the first time. Someone who, if I follow their lead, may nudge me toward those many other lives I could lead. They're wounded and bruised from what has just happened to them, soon to be scarred by the world—and the person—they're leaving behind. They're urging me to get closer to and look closer at them. They're my stranger. They want me to jump.

I can't say I've successfully approximated Natalie Portman's (or Manet's barmaid's, let alone Toor's bartender's) seductive stare. But that's not stopped me from trying every morning as I look at myself in the mirror and mouth the two words that serve now as a balm, as a call, as a mission:

"Hello, stranger."

ACKNOWLEDGMENTS

The very tenets of this book would not have been possible without the love, support, and patience of two men who helped rewire me in ways I'm still sorting through. Joe, Ami, I owe the world to you. I am who I am today because of you, and *Hello Stranger* is a testament to the kind of intimacies you've built, modeled, and reconstituted for and around me. I cannot thank you both enough.

In matters more germane to the world of publishing, I want to thank, first and foremost, my agent, Michael Bourret. While he was right to worry this was bound to be quite a painful book to write, he was steadfast in his support, trusting that I could find a way through it. And to my editor, Alicia Kroell, who saw potential in the seedling of an idea I first presented to her and helped shape that project into this much more ambitious book you now hold in your hands. Thank you, both, for nudging me to think bigger and to go bolder. I am very lucky to have had you both alongside me to shepherd these "musings" out into the world. And thank you to the entire Catapult team, who have been so great to work with and who, once again, gifted me with the sexiest cover a queer writer could dream of. Thank you, as well, to Matt Ortile (at *Catapult* magazine) and to Tracy O'Neill (at *Epiphany* magazine) for publishing essays that soon became, in decidedly different forms, integral to *Hello Stranger.*

I've always been quite a solitary—if not outright lonely—writer. But there are friendships that sustain me and help make this make-shift writerly life all the more bearable. So thank you to Steven Rowley, Byron Lane, Thad Nurski, Jack Smart, Jeff Ling, Peggy Truong, Francisco Chacin, Tony Rodriguez, Isaac Tintó, Kyle Buchanan, Greg Ellwood, and many, many more, including the many friends and acquaintances online (on Insta and Twitter/X and all those various other apps) whose DMs have made for great research and even greater comfort. Thanks as well to John MacConnell, whose artistry and friendship for more than a decade serves as the key inspiration for my chapter on figure drawing.

And, finally, thank you to all those strangers I've encountered over the years—and the many more I'm sure to meet in the years to come.

© Jack Manning

MANUEL BETANCOURT is a queer Colombian culture writer and film critic. His work has been featured in *The New York Times, BuzzFeed News, Los Angeles Times, Film Quarterly, Los Angeles Review of Books, GQ,* and other publications. Betancourt is the author of *The Male Gazed: On Hunks, Heartthrobs, and What Pop Culture Taught Me About (Desiring) Men* and *Judy Garland's "Judy at Carnegie Hall,"* and he is a contributing writer to the Eisner Award–nominated graphic novel series The Cardboard Kingdom.